"Reading *Mere Evangeli...* [barcode obscures text] ...y a genius to help me unlo [barcode obscures text] ...ris- tian friends! It really wa [barcode obscures text] ...us book that trains me for e [barcode obscures text] ...he first paragraph of chapter [barcode obscures text]

**RICO TICE, S** ...is Church, Langham Place, London

"One of the most helpful, concise, and inspiring books on evangelism I've read. Using C.S. Lewis's winsome rhetoric and joy-based apologetics as a model, Newman offers a roadmap for effective evangelism in a secular age—one that engages the head and the heart to persuade skeptics that the gospel is too beautiful and too good not to be true."

**BRETT MCCRACKEN, Senior Editor, The Gospel Coalition; Author, *The Wisdom Pyramid: Feeding Your Soul in a Post-Truth World***

"Every Christian willing to admit that evangelism is difficult will identify with Randy and benefit from his well-written study of C.S. Lewis's strategies and biblical teaching on this topic. He comes alongside us to offer practical application steps that lead to conversations about God and the gospel, and motivate us to share the good news with the people around us."

**LIN JOHNSON, Director, Write-to-Publish Conference**

"Not since Manley Pippert's *Out of the Saltshaker* and Chapman's *Know and Tell the Gospel* has a book on evangelism so captured my imagination and warmed my heart. In *Mere Evangelism* the intertwining of the imaginative apologetic of C.S. Lewis and biblical principles is unique and masterly. Newman highlights the brilliance of Lewis without eulogising and is careful to ensure that the book is replete with Scripture. *Mere Evangelism* will prove a tremendous resource in helping Christians to spread the aroma of the knowledge of Christ everywhere."

**EDWIN EWART, Principal, Irish Baptist College**

"I have been waiting for a book like this for years. *Mere Evangelism* in-troduces the work of C.S. Lewis, equips us in evangelism and educates us about today's ever-changing culture. I didn't anticipate it being better than Randy's *Questioning Evangelism*. It is! If C.S. Lewis is the 'steak' of apologetics, this book is the new go-to plate, knife, fork, French fries, salad and sauce. There simply isn't another book quite like it."

**MITCH CROWN, Evangelist; Co-founder, Crown Jesus Ministries**

"A first-rate book on personal evangelism. No modern Christian in the English-speaking world has reached as many people with the gospel as C.S. Lewis, and Dr. Newman provides the reader with ten insights on how Professor Lewis fulfilled the Great Commission."

**DR. LYLE DORSETT, former Director, The Marion E. Wade Center, Wheaton College**

"Randy doesn't pretend evangelism is easy. In fact, he states the opposite. But even if he can't make it magically easy, he does make it desirable and realistic. His blend of experience, clarity, and contagiousness make him compelling like few others on this topic. Randy's writing will help break the spell the secular age is trying to cast on us to keep us quiet about Jesus. Perhaps this book is just what you need for the post-COVID world and its new evangelistic opportunities."

**DAVID MATHIS, Executive Editor, desiringGod.org**

"Conversion, C.S. Lewis once remarked, 'does not occur without the intervention of the supernatural'. He knew that only the mysterious action of divine grace can finally change someone's heart, and his humility before that mystery underpinned all the extraordinary efforts in evangelism that characterised his life and work. *Mere Evangelism* examines Lewis's example in a thorough and thoughtful manner and reflects the same spirit of humility. I warmly recommend it."

**DR. MICHAEL WARD, Fellow of Blackfriars Hall, University of Oxford; Professor of Apologetics, Houston Baptist University; Author, *After Humanity: A Guide to C.S. Lewis's The Abolition of Man***

"Most of the time, evangelism does not take place in a single conversation. It is a process of bringing the truth of the gospel into an encounter with someone in need of grace. Using C.S. Lewis as a shining example, Randy Newman takes us through this process. *Mere Evangelism* is a wonderful resource, full not only of evangelistic principles but also of evangelistic passion."

**TREVIN WAX, Author, *This Is Our Time***

"Dr. Randy Newman has pulled off a rare feat. He's written a book on evangelism that is both practical and beautiful. He adeptly pulls out valuable insights from the writings and life of C.S. Lewis on how to be an effective witness for Christ, yet does so with imagination and grace-full prose. If you desire to tell others about Jesus, this book will help you tremendously. Read it and prayerfully apply its principles, and I know that others will be drawn 'further up and further in.'"

**DR. JOEL WOODRUFF, President, The C.S. Lewis Institute**

"A beautiful book that weaves together the best of C.S. Lewis's creative storytelling and wisdom with Newman's vast experience and theological underpinning for evangelism. It culminates in a wonderfully well-rounded and easily accessible book that leaves you feeling more joy in the gospel yourself and excited about taking the gospel to those around you."

**CHRIS MCBURNEY, Christian Unions Ireland**

"This book challenged, refreshed, and inspired me. Randy Newman is a compelling guide and writes with clarity. He does more than tell us to share the good news—he makes us want to do it and helps us become better at it."

"I have read quite a few books on evangelism (including more than a few by this author), but this stands out. Newman performs a real service to the reader by mining the riches of C.S. Lewis's works and making them immediately applicable to the gospel conversations we are having (or wanting to have) with our friends and family every day. As I read, I found myself informed, encouraged, and excited to engage more people with the good news. I have no doubt that I will often have occasion to recommend this book to others."

"Randy Newman has done it again—but even better than before. His descriptive prowess and ability to turn a phrase shed new light on the passion, burden, and intelligence of C.S. Lewis's arguments for the faith. A must-read for all who are committed to proclaiming the gospel today."

"*Mere Evangelism* combines an articulation of C.S. Lewis's art of translating the Christian faith in ways that make sense to the ordinary outsider with a realistic approach to evangelism from our current starting point in an increasingly secular world. Shaped by its insights, we will be better equipped to accompany the Spirit's work in nudging others along on their journey to Jesus."

"Randy Newman has dug deeply into Lewis's works to unearth and display treasures that are often overlooked. Throughout, he sprinkles the text with helpful tips that will both motivate us and help us more effectively engage our friends with the message of the gospel."

"C.S. Lewis wrote, 'If Christianity is untrue, then no honest man will want to believe it … if it is true, every honest man will want to believe it.' From that secure footing, Randy Newman's highly readable book translates Lewis's approach to evangelism effectively for today's contemporary audiences."

RANDY NEWMAN

*Mere Evangelism*

thegoodbook
COMPANY

Mere Evangelism
© Randy Newman 2021

Published by:
The Good Book Company

thegoodbook.com | thegoodbook.co.uk
thegoodbook.com.au | thegoodbook.co.nz | thegoodbook.co.in

ISBN: 9781784986445 | Printed in Turkey

Design by André Parker

*To Pam,*

*my joy,*

*and co-heir of the gracious gift of life.*

# CONTENTS

# FOREWORD

M*ere Christianity*, yes, we all know about C.S. Lewis's book with that title, spun out of some BBC radio talks during WWII; but *Mere Evangelism*? Does C.S. Lewis have anything to teach us about evangelism—let alone ten insights?

If Lewis were alive today, I suspect he might be surprised at our surprise, for in his view of his own work, all his popular Christian writing was driven, at least in part, by evangelistic concerns. By this I mean that what he said and how he said it were shaped by his understanding of the gospel, and how to be winsome and persuasive in articulating it. Once you become aware of this fundamental feature of his work, and start looking for it, it is not hard to find, whether in overtly evangelistic essays (like *Mere Christianity*), works of beguiling fantasy (like the *Narnia* set), sober treatments of objections to Christian faith (like *The Problem of Pain*), or rather personal testimony (like *A Grief Observed*).

True, Lewis never set out to teach a course on evangelism or apologetics. Rather, it is the manner in which he writes that testifies to his self-conscious awareness of the importance of winsomely disclosing Christian truth. In this book, Randy Newman is careful not to over-schematize Lewis. He does not pretend that Lewis set out to deliver these "ten insights," still less construe them as ten lessons. Rather, Newman's book is the result of a close, inductive reading of Lewis, while asking the kinds of questions that a seasoned evangelist like Randy Newman cannot help but pose. The ten insights are overtly the thought of Randy Newman, but they are laced with so many telling examples drawn from the corpus of C.S. Lewis that they are overtly the thought of Lewis, too.

The result is more than a primer on evangelism, but not exactly an advanced course on the subject, either. Rather, while providing a stimulating entré into the thought of C.S. Lewis, Randy Newman has given us a refresher course on evangelism, graced with the lightness of touch and imagination characteristic of Lewis himself.

D.A. Carson

# INTRODUCTION

I magine you're sitting on a bus with a book by C.S. Lewis—let's say one of his *Narnia* volumes—and someone asks you what you're reading.

When you respond to your new acquaintance, her face lights up, and she tells you she read *The Chronicles of Narnia* when she was a child. She asks which is your favorite in the series, and a fun conversation ensues. Then, "Do you know his other books?" she wonders. "Didn't he write about religion or something?"

Would you know what to say? Could you point her beyond Aslan?

Or suppose you're attending your cousin's wedding and you meet a relative you haven't seen in decades. He shakes your hand, asks how you've been, and then says, "I've heard you've become religious. How'd that happen?"

Are you prepared for such a question? Or do you hope the band starts to play something really loud?

Evangelism is an extraordinary task; it's what God uses to bring people from death to life. But it is difficult. It always has been. We need inspiration and help—and I can think of no better source of those things (humanly speaking, anyway) than the creator of Narnia, C.S. Lewis: a man who has been used by God to point countless wanderers to the one who promised eternal life.

## SURPRISED BY LEWIS

A decade before he published the *Narnia* books, Lewis was well known for his *Broadcast Talks*, a BBC radio series which presented the Christian faith to listeners across the UK. This was the material which later became the book *Mere Christianity*—ensuring that Lewis's evangelistic influence did not last just in his own lifetime. When *Christianity Today* magazine "asked more than 100 of its contributors and church leaders to nominate the ten best religious books of the twentieth century ... by far, C.S. Lewis was the most popular author and *Mere Christianity* the book nominated most often."[1]

Quite apart from the content of the *Broadcast Talks*—which we'll come to later—the story of how they came about should itself energize us for evangelism. It was less than a year after Britain had sustained nightly onslaughts of bombing by the Nazis and only a short time after the miracle of Dunkirk. At this desperate moment, producers at the BBC invited Lewis to craft short messages about the Christian faith to be woven into the weekly programing.

The original plan offered five messages of less than fifteen minutes each, one week apart, from August 6th to September 6th, 1941. These attracted enough listeners to warrant a second series, also of five messages, four months later. A third and then a fourth series were commissioned. From beginning to end, these broadcasts took almost three years! We might learn something from this about perseverance through gradual evangelism.

But the most amazing thing was the unlikely size of the audience. You might enjoy hearing about what fare preceded Lewis's messages at 7:45 pm. "At 7pm came a half-hour variety show of musical acts by less-than-impressive amateurs—[with] such improbably named groups as the Berkeley Square Bunkhouse Singers and the Hillbilly Swingers."[2] At 7:15 came the news—"not in English or even in Welsh but in Norwegian."[3] If ever an audience had a good excuse to turn off their radios, fifteen minutes of news in a foreign language was it. And yet, people did *not* turn off. They listened—over 1.2 million of them, week after week, over the course of months and years.

Longtime friend and biographer of Lewis, George Sayer, remembered "being at a pub filled with soldiers on one Wednesday evening. At a quarter to eight, the bartender turned the radio up for Lewis. 'You listen to this bloke,' he shouted. 'He's really worth listening to.' And those soldiers did listen attentively for the entire fifteen minutes."[4] We could learn something about trusting a supernatural God for supernatural results by remembering stories like these.

## ANOTHER RELUCTANT CONVERT

Because Lewis was a writer as well as a broadcaster, his evangelistic influence has extended far beyond his own times. I know this firsthand: his words were instrumental in my own journey to faith.

Growing up in a Jewish home, I heard very little about Jesus. Religion meant reciting prayers, participating in rituals, and celebrating holidays. To me, the Almighty seemed distant and alien. So, in my first year of college—aided by existentialist writers, Woody Allen movies, Kurt Vonnegut novels, and parties with large quantities of beer—I decided life was just absurd; it would never really make sense.

But even though I believed life was meaningless, I desperately hoped I would find something to prove that theory wrong. I loved music: perhaps that could provide the link to the transcendent, a connection to something beyond the material world. But every piece of music disappointed, every concert ended, and every noisy subway ride back to my dorm room contrasted rudely with the splendors of Dvorak, Rachmaninoff, and Mozart.

Little did I know, however, that I was already on a journey to saving faith.

Back in high school, one of my drinking buddies had invited me to his church's youth group because, he said, "the girls are cute." He was right, and I became a regular, albeit non-Christian, attender of that youth group's many activities. Along the way, I heard the gospel—a message I promptly dismissed as "something Christians should believe" but irrelevant to Jewish people because "Jews don't believe in Jesus."

But people at that youth group displayed a kind of relationship with God that I found attractive. They prayed about anything and everything, and urged me to read the New Testament, as well as a book by some English guy named C.S. Lewis. I read neither. But I remembered the title of the book: *Mere Christianity.* And oddly, several years later, as I got ready for my sophomore year of college, I shoved the New Testament into one of my packing boxes.

It remained in my closet as I resumed my absurd-reading, beer-drinking, concert-attending rituals. Then all that came to a screeching halt when a friend died in a tragic accident. Sitting at his funeral, I realized that Woody, Kurt, and Heineken could not provide the answers I longed for. "If there is a god, how can I know him?" I wondered. I went back to my dorm room and started reading that New Testament. I also checked out *Mere Christianity* from the library. I read both where nobody could see me.

As I read Matthew's quotations from the Old Testament and Jesus' claims to be God, C.S. Lewis's arguments stoked my searching. He eliminated one of my firmest convictions—that Jesus was just a good teacher. I'll never forget reading, "A man who was merely a man and said the sort of things Jesus said would not be a great moral teacher. He would either be a lunatic—on a level with the man who says he is a poached egg—or else he would be the Devil of Hell. You must make your choice. Either this man was, and is, the Son of God: or else a madman or something worse."[5]

That convinced me that Jesus was the Messiah. But mere intellectual assent has never saved anyone. It was the other strand of Lewis's presentation that pushed me over the line of surrender. When I got to his chapter on hope, I saw why every concert left me feeling empty. After offering "two wrong ways" of dealing with life's disappointments, Lewis wrote, "If I find in myself a desire which no experience in this world can satisfy, the most probable explanation is that I was made for another world."[6]

It was at the intersection of the intellect (Jesus was who he said he was) and imagination (I was made for another world) that the gospel became irresistible to me. Sitting at my dormitory desk, I acknowledged that Jesus was not just *the* Messiah but *my* Messiah, the one I longed for in music and needed for atonement for my sins. Unlike Lewis, who said he came to believe in God "kicking, struggling, resentful … perhaps, that night, the most dejected and reluctant convert in all England," I rejoiced with singing.[7] It felt like a tremendous relief to receive music as a gift and not demand it be a god—and to have no need to perform rituals because I could rest in the finished work of the cross. I was overjoyed.

It's the intertwining of the two forces of mind and imagination that, I believe, made C.S. Lewis such a powerful evangelist, not only for me but for countless others. An expert on medieval literature may not seem like the kind of person God would use for widespread evangelistic fruit. But Lewis saw himself as a "translator—one turning Christian doctrine … into language that unscholarly people would attend to and could understand."[8]

People listened to Lewis not because of his impressive qualifications but because he spoke in ways that made sense to them. We read his fiction today because it takes us to a land beyond a wardrobe. He appeals to our whole selves.

Lewis firmly believed that "most of my books are evangelistic".[9] That's why it's not only *Mere Christianity* but also his many other writings that we can learn from as we seek inspiration for evangelism. As part of my work, I once conducted extensive interviews of students about their conversions. Unsurprisingly, Lewis's writings were mentioned frequently: not only *Mere Christianity* but *The Chronicles of Narnia* and his other fiction, as well as apologetic works like *Miracles* and essays like *The Weight of Glory*. All these helped nudge people out of skepticism into faith. In one instance, it was a movie version of *The Voyage of the Dawn Treader* that ushered a theater major across the line of belief.

It's with stories like those in mind that I write this book. By unpacking how this one far-from-ordinary evangelist did outreach, I believe we can equip ourselves in new ways for the extraordinary task of evangelism.

## ALL THE ROAD BEFORE US

You may feel inadequate to the task. There is only one C.S. Lewis. But the methods he used—storytelling, imagery, directness and humor, to name just a few—are all tools we can pick up and apply in our own conversations.

Each chapter that follows weaves together an approach Lewis used and some ways we can practice it, as well as thoughts about how Scripture sheds light on those methods. The third of those considerations is by far the most important. C.S. Lewis did many things well, but let's face it: he wasn't perfect. God's word is our flawless authority and the best resource to help us evangelize.

After all, our greatest "qualification" is not in ourselves—it's in the self-authenticating, powerful truth of our message. We can be "not ashamed of the gospel, because it is the power of

God that brings salvation to everyone who believes" (Romans 1 v 16).

Evangelism occurs at the intersection of the human and the divine, the natural and the supernatural, the practical and the impossible. God calls timid Timothys to "do the work of an evangelist" (2 Timothy 4 v 5). Flawed, reluctant, sinful, less-than-brilliant proclaimers contribute the human ingredients—making "the most of every opportunity," letting our "conversation be always full of grace" and "seasoned with salt" (Colossians 4 v 5-6). Then God provides what no human evangelist can—opening up blind eyes, softening hardened hearts, and drawing people to himself. That's how it worked with Lewis's *Broadcast Talks*. That's how it worked in my own journey to faith. And that's how it will work for all of us.

This isn't a book to increase membership in a C.S. Lewis fan club or prompt praise for him. It's to strengthen our resolve to point lost people to the one who can deliver them from a realm where it's "always winter but never Christmas." My prayer is that this book will help you say and do things that will make an eternal difference in many people's lives.

When C.S. Lewis was writing *The Four Loves*—which is not considered a particularly evangelistic book—he still had a posture toward outreach. He wrote to a friend, "Pray for me that God grant me to say things helpful to salvation, or at least not harmful."[10]

May we all have that same mindset and prayer.

# 1. THE NECESSITY OF
# PRE-EVANGELISM

Before Tom Tarrants assumed the role of President of the C.S. Lewis Institute, he co-pastored a multi-racial church in ethnically diverse Washington, D.C. Before that, he was a seminary student. Before that, he blew up buildings—or, at least, he tried to. He particularly targeted the properties of Jews and Blacks, the groups he hated most (although Roman Catholics were high on that list as well). That's why he joined the Ku Klux Klan. This partly explains how he landed in a state penitentiary. He escaped, got recaptured, was sent back to solitary confinement in that same prison, and, in a six foot by nine foot windowless prison cell, became a Christian.

As you might guess, I've left out a few details of his story, which is told rivetingly in his book *Consumed by Hate: Redeemed by Love.* An aspect of the story I find intriguing is that before he came to faith, he read books on philosophy. For months, he worked through weighty philosophical works by the likes of Hegel, Plato, Aristotle, and the Stoics.[11] It was as if he needed his thinking about truth in general rewired before exploring the specific truth of the gospel. It was through reading a book on political philosophy that he began questioning his views about race. He came to see he was wrong about something he had felt so right about—the inferiority of some races to others. Realigning his thinking about truth paved the way for him to submit to *the* truth.

Not everyone needs to read Plato before Paul. But some do.

Joy Davidman, who later became C.S. Lewis's wife, had to have her thinking about communist doctrine debunked before she could entertain another doctrine—the Christian one. She also had to realize that she "believed in science the way religious people believe in God." The painful events of World War II exposed flaws in Marxism and atheism that opened her up to consider theism. She admitted that her previously held beliefs were "hopeless" and "naïve."[12]

Both Tom and Joy encountered what many call pre-evangelism: a preparation for receiving the gospel. This preparation can take a much wider variety of forms than we see in those first two examples (so don't be put off if they seem a little highbrow). Most people need a less academic version—challenges to their lifestyles or morality, perhaps. But I am convinced that for our current context, pre-evangelism may be the most important and least valued strategy for fruitful evangelism.[13] I also believe it is the most important lesson we can learn from C.S. Lewis. That's why I put this chapter first.

## PAVING THE WAY

You may be resistant to this idea. You may be thinking, "Can't we just preach the simple gospel and let God do the rest?" I understand the concern for not compromising the gospel. But consider that Jesus and Paul both modeled pre-evangelism before expounding the specifics of the cross and resurrection.

To the woman at the well, Jesus spent a fair amount of time talking about water and thirst, appealing first to her *desires*. He spoke about a thirst that could not be satisfied through relationships. In her case, it was seen in five failed marriages and a current cohabitation with a similarly doomed prospect.

Sometimes, we need to point out to people that they've fashioned broken cisterns that can't hold water (see Jeremiah 2 v 13) before we offer living water.

With the Stoic and Epicurean philosophers on Mars Hill in Athens, Paul gave a lot of attention to the nature of knowledge and what it means to be human, appealing to their *intellect*.

His speech explored what people can know about God through general revelation. He urged his listeners to consider people's efforts to reach beyond themselves (their "objects of worship," Acts 17 v 23) and to recall what their poets had already expressed (the idea that "we are his offspring," v 28).

Paul's flow of logic in Romans 1 and 2 echoes the same progression. We see God's general revelation in nature (Romans 1 v 20) and in our consciences (2 v 15) before the clear statement of the gospel in the Scriptures (3 v 21-26). Sometimes the set-up is as important as the delivery.

In John Stott's insightful commentary on Paul's methodology, he pointed out:

> *"The Areopagus [Mars Hill] address reveals the comprehensiveness of Paul's message. He proclaimed God in his fullness as Creator, Sustainer, Ruler, Father and Judge ... Now all this is part of the gospel. Or at least it is the indispensable background to the gospel, without which the gospel cannot effectively be preached. Many people are rejecting our gospel today not because they perceive it to be false, but because they perceive it to be trivial. People are looking for an integrated world-view which makes sense of all their experience. We learn from Paul that we cannot preach the gospel of Jesus without the doctrine of God, or the cross without the creation, or salvation without judgment."* [14]

I hope you'll see by now what I mean when I say "pre-evangelism" and "evangelism." By "evangelism," I mean a very precise, rather narrow task—the verbal proclamation of the gospel message. This message is that God has a kingdom and we can become citizens of that kingdom, all because of Jesus' death and resurrection. (I'll say a great deal more about this message and how we can proclaim it clearly in chapter 5.) By "pre-evangelism," I mean a wide array of conversations and actions that pave the way and build plausibility for understanding and reception of the gospel. Jesus' conversation about thirst; Paul's quotation from a Greek poet; the breaking-down of Tom Tarrants's prejudices with the help of books on philosophy—all these are pre-evangelism.

## PREPARATION FOR GOOD NEWS

Here's how C.S. Lewis began his very first *Broadcast Talk:* "Every one has heard people quarreling."[15] He goes on to argue that we all have some sense of right and wrong, and that is a "clue to the meaning of the universe."[16] He doesn't start with Jesus. He begins by appealing to a sense of right and wrong.

Being an academic, Lewis used Latin to describe his methods. "Mine are *praeparatio evangelica* [a preparation for good news] rather than *evangelium* [the good news itself]." Lewis's preparation consisted in an attempt to convince people that "there is a moral law, that we disobey it, and that the existence of a Lawgiver is at least very probable and also (unless you add the Christian doctrine of the Atonement) that this imparts despair rather than comfort."[17]

This was no minor consideration for Lewis. He reiterated it many times and in many ways as a non-negotiable starting point. In a letter to the BBC proposing his strategy for the broadcasts, he wrote, "I think what I mainly want to talk about is the Law of Nature, or objective right and wrong. It seems to me that the N[ew] T[estament], by preaching repentance and forgiveness, always *assumes* an audience who already believe in the law of Nature and know they have disobeyed it. In modern England we cannot at present assume this, and therefore most apologetic begins a stage too far on. The first step is to create, or recover, the sense of guilt."[18]

(Note: The New Testament does not "always" assume this. Lewis's point still stands, but his observation about the New Testament needs fine tuning.)

When Lewis was offering advice to would-be evangelists, he observed, "The greatest barrier I have met is the almost total absence from the minds of my audience of any sense of sin."[19] But he also saw numerous other obstacles to overcome or assumptions to challenge. People distrusted authority.[20] They thought Christians only believed what they did because they "liked it" rather than because they believed it to be true.[21] Many people stood in judgment over God instead of accepting their need for submission to him.

And if these concerns applied to Britain in the 1940s, they seem even more pertinent today.

People's presuppositions—their underlying, often unspoken beliefs about themselves, God, and the world—either set them up for belief in the gospel or for the rejection of it. Some assumptions pave the way for acceptance. Others need to be torn down.

For example, if someone's presupposition is that they themselves are the source of all truth and they merely need to look within to find answers, it may be difficult for them to consider any outside source as a higher authority. This means that merely quoting the Bible to them may not be the best starting point. Instead, pointing out contradictions within their own thinking could help. Or we can help them admit that some of what comes from within is not good—for them or for the people around them. We may need to blast before we can build. I'll say more about this in chapters 3 and 4.

On one occasion, Lewis remarked, "When grave persons express their fear that England is relapsing into Paganism, I am tempted to reply, 'Would that she were'... For a Pagan, as history shows, is a man eminently convertible to Christianity. He is essentially the pre-Christian, or sub-Christian, religious man ... The Christian and the Pagan have much more in common with one another than either has with the writers of the *New Statesman*."[22] We need to recognize that today's secularist may be tougher to win to Christ than people who call themselves "spiritual but not religious." Their belief in the supernatural, albeit some pretty bizarre varieties of it, may be a better starting point than a hard-boiled naturalist's exclusive dependence on science.

Lewis's emphasis on first preparing the way for the gospel gave shape to his series of radio messages. Consider how many individual broadcasts people had heard before he started talking about Jesus. At the end of his fourth message, he admitted, "Do not think I am going faster than I really am. I am not yet within a hundred miles of the God of Christian theology."[23] Even in the second series of messages, he stuck to discussing how we know things in the first place (epistemology) before venturing into what we know about God (theology) or what we should believe about Jesus (Christology).

One significant difference between *Mere Christianity* and most evangelistic books is that the other ones tell readers what to believe and why they should believe it. Lewis's work paves the way for belief by removing obstacles and painting images of what belief is like.

Do not conclude that Lewis undervalued the importance of direct, non-nuanced evangelism. He saw the need for both sowing and reaping but recognized that his giftedness lay on the sowing side. He saw the balance this way: "I am not sure that the ideal missionary team ought not to consist of one who argues and one who (in the fullest sense of the word) preaches. Put up your arguer first to undermine their intellectual prejudices; then let the evangelist proper launch his appeal."[24]

Think of the way pitching in Major League baseball has evolved. Today, very few starting pitchers finish games they begin. But that was not always the case. Records for complete games will probably never be broken because of how the game has changed. Today, we hope a starting pitcher makes it to the sixth or seventh inning, when a set-up man comes in for one or two innings and then the game is completed by a closer. They each play their role. They each pitch differently. They have different expertise. Together they win games.

Think about your own role in evangelism and pre-evangelism. What kind of "pitcher" are you? Are you most comfortable as a set-up man or woman? Or do your gifts lie in launching a direct appeal with an outline of the gospel message? Perhaps you're not sure you are all that good at either. My aim in this book is to help you to improve your game in both roles.

## A GRADUAL ROAD

Perhaps Lewis valued pre-evangelism because of his own gradual path to conversion. He needed roadblocks to be dismantled before he could seriously consider the gospel.

Some of those objections were more emotional than intellectual. Recounting his reading of 19th-century writer George MacDonald's fantasy novel *Phantastes*, he said, "That night my imagination was, in a certain sense, baptized; the rest of me, not unnaturally, took longer."[25] MacDonald's Christian-based mythology shook up Lewis's love of Norse mythology. This first wave started in his affections. Then a second wave went after his intellect. After *Phantastes* came the conversations with fellow writer J.R.R. Tolkien and others, which changed Lewis's thinking.

Actually, that second wave was a series of waves. Lewis moved first from atheism to theism and only later to Christian theism. The first part felt far from pleasant. (Remember his famous "most reluctant convert" description?) Logic convinced Lewis that he had no basis for objecting to suffering and no reason to be drawn to beauty if there was no God and the world had no meaning. He admitted, "Nearly all that I loved I believed to be imaginary. Nearly all that I believed to be real I thought grim and meaningless."[26]

Then came his pivotal conversation with J.R.R. Tolkien and Hugo Dyson (another academic and writer) as they circled for hours around Addison's Walk, a wooded path at Magdalen College in Oxford. In a letter to his lifelong friend Arthur Greeves, Lewis summed up that fateful night:

> "Now what Dyson and Tolkien showed me was this: That if I met the idea of sacrifice in a Pagan story I didn't mind it at all: again, that if I met the idea of a god sacrificing himself to himself ... I liked it very much and was mysteriously moved by it ... The reason was that in Pagan stories I was prepared to feel the myth as profound and suggestive of meanings beyond my grasp even though I could not say in cold prose 'what it meant.' Now the story of Christ is simply a true myth: a myth working on us in the same way as the others, but with this tremendous difference that it really happened..." [27]

It was in a letter to Arthur just a few days before this when Lewis first acknowledged, "I have just passed on from believing in God to definitely believing in Christ—in Christianity. I will try to explain this another time. My long night talk with Dyson and Tolkien had a good deal to do with it."[28]

While Lewis described his initial move from atheism to

theism as "darting his eyes in every direction for a chance of escape," his move to saving faith in Jesus seemed ordinary. "I know very well when, but hardly how, the final step was taken. I was driven to Whipsnade one sunny morning. When we set out I did not believe that Jesus Christ is the Son of God, and when we reached the zoo I did."[29]

Perhaps Lewis appreciated the need for pre-evangelism so much because it was the route he took in his own conversion. Many people today need the same roadmap.

## SOWING AND REAPING

But how exactly *do* pre-evangelism and evangelism fit together? Where does one finish and the other start? Jesus' teaching about sowing and reaping can help.

Both processes are necessary for a harvest. But they're not the same.[30] After Jesus demonstrated sowing in his conversation with the woman at the well, we hear him teach about it:

> *"My food," said Jesus, "is to do the will of him who sent me and to finish his work. Don't you have a saying, 'It's still four months until harvest'? I tell you, open your eyes and look at the fields! They are ripe for harvest. Even now the one who reaps draws a wage and harvests a crop for eternal life, so that the sower and the reaper may be glad together. Thus the saying 'One sows and another reaps' is true. I sent you to reap what you have not worked for. Others have done the hard work, and you have reaped the benefits of their labor." (John 4 v 34-38)*

There are four key points. First, the different tasks of sowing and reaping may be accomplished by different people. Second, Jesus calls sowing "the hard work." Third, reapers benefit from the work done by others before they pursue their task. Fourth, we can expect the dual process to yield joyful results.

Over twenty years ago, author Tim Downs imagined a real-life farmer who loves the reaping part of the task but finds the "hard work" of sowing (breaking up hard ground, pulling weeds, removing rocks, tilling the soil, mixing in fertilizer, sorting out bad seed, working the seed into the soil, and probably a dozen other tasks non-agrarians can't even imagine) annoyingly bothersome. So, he skips the sowing part and waits for the fun part of reaping. Absurd, isn't it? Downs warned, "In our zeal for the harvest, we have forgotten—we have deliberately *devalued*—the role of those who sow in our generation."[31]

Pre-evangelism is part of the task of sowing. All that preparatory work is vital if we want to see our seeds bear gospel fruit.

So much more can be said in support of pre-evangelism. A case could be made that the entire Old Testament is pre-evangelistic. Promises of a Messiah—direct predictions, foreshadowings, or subtle hints—all prepare the way for reception when he finally arrives. We'll talk more about this in later chapters. But let's turn now to consider ways in which we ourselves can pre-evangelize.

## A NEW WAY OF SEEING

Learning the skill of pre-evangelism (and it is indeed a skill to be developed—but, encouragingly, not all that difficult a skill) begins by seeing how God paved the way for our own salvation through conversations, actions, and hints long before we arrived at rebirth.

Think back. Can you recall specific people who said things to you that challenged your assumptions? Do you remember reading something that sparked your wonder about a world that's better than our current version? Perhaps there was a song or a story or a movie that stimulated a longing for release. Or were there conversations about philosophical or theoretical issues that engaged your thinking about bigger issues than you had ever considered?

If you were raised in a Christian family, perhaps you can see evidence of pre-evangelism in your parents' or grandparents' lives. Or maybe you can look for displays of God's preparation in the lives of other Christians.

For many people, it takes a while to remember details or connect seemingly disparate events. When I listen to people's conversion narratives, I deliberately allow at least 45 minutes. It takes that long for many people to draw together important components of their story. To be sure, in our evangelism, we need to keep the sharing of our testimonies brief—one to three minutes max. But when we examine God's manifold grace privately or with other Christians, we would do well to linger longer. Why not make this a feature of your church's community group, taking turns to share conversion stories and allowing each other to draw out details you may have long forgotten?

Once you have collected some memories of ways in which God worked pre-evangelistically in your own life and the lives of other Christians, start brainstorming some sowing conversations you might have with a non-Christian you know. Those memories should give you some ideas; what are the similarities between your non-Christian friends and your own pre-converted self (or parent or friend)? How could you help them take steps down the road you took?

Here's another simple way of starting a pre-evangelistic conversation: pick just one person and just one aspect of God's world to discuss. If they love art and beauty, point them to the one who made our world so beautiful. If they value family, explore how God made us to be social beings. We can drop ideas like these into our conversations, one at a time—there's no need to make a big deal of it at first. But let's ask God to develop these Mars Hill conversations into discussions of Jesus' death and resurrection (which is the ultimate destination of Paul's presentation, by the way; see Acts 17 v 31).

These exercises are just a start. We'll explore more pre-evangelistic strategies as we move forward in the chapters ahead.

For Lewis, pre-evangelism came in the form of a conversation about myth. For me, it was a sequence of beautiful, yet disappointing concerts. For my friend Tom, it was philosophy. What was it for you? What might it be for your friends? Look for conversation starters in ordinary experiences and see how God might use them in extraordinary ways.

# 2. THE APPEAL
# TO CLUES

I f you ever have the joy of visiting Belfast, Northern Ireland, you can take a tour of important sites in C.S. Lewis's life, including his boyhood home, Little Lea, which inspired visions of Narnia, Campbell College (with a prominent lamppost near the entrance), his grandfather's church (with a lion-shaped doorknocker), and other spots that expand your appreciation of him. On most guided and self-guided tours, people make a stop at Dundela, the house where he was born—and it usually disappoints.

The original structure that was the first Lewis home was torn down in 1953 and replaced with a nondescript apartment building. On the side of the building, a small, round plaque reads, "C.S. Lewis, 1898-1963, Author and Christian Apologist, born on this site." It is the only evidence of any connection between the author and that location. Given the difficulties of finding the place, the lack of sufficient parking, and the need to cross a busy street to see the plaque, many people wonder if it was worth the trouble.

But not those who participate in tours led by Sandy Smith, long-time resident of Belfast and C.S. Lewis aficionado. Sandy weaves in entertaining stories, humorous anecdotes, and memorized quotes from *Surprised by Joy* and *The Chronicles of Narnia*, making you wish he could go on for hours. Indeed, when my tour group heard him speak, standing underneath that small, round plaque, we listened intently as he talked about Lewis's first memory of joy.

Lewis called joy "the central story of my life."[32] But don't think of it as a kind of happiness. In a variety of places, he described it as a kind of desirable ache, "a lifelong nostalgia," what German speakers call *Sehnsucht*.[33] People feel it when they see something beautiful or hear a piece of music that transports them to another world. They get a hint of it when they read a story that makes them want to jump into the book and never return. Hard to describe, it's more of an experience than an idea—more a fleeting sensation than a conscious realization. Lewis observed, "We usually notice it just as the moment of vision dies away, as the music ends, or as the landscape loses the celestial light."[34] He gave it an expansive description in his sermon "The Weight of Glory," as "the scent of a flower we have not found, the echo of a tune we have not heard, news from a country we have never yet visited."[35] He defined joy as "an unsatisfied desire which is itself more desirable than any satisfaction."[36]

Lewis called it joy. I tend to think of it as longing. It's a desire in our hearts we can't ignore but also can't satisfy—at least not in this world. To understand C.S. Lewis, you must understand joy. And, for the purposes of this book, understanding joy can open up marvelous opportunities to connect searchers for joy with the Source of all joy.

When Sandy Smith stood below that small, round plaque, he recounted a story Lewis told in the opening pages of *Surprised by Joy*. His brother, Warnie, came into the nursery with "a biscuit tin which he had covered with moss and garnished with twigs and flowers so as to make it a toy garden or a toy forest." Their family either did not value art or couldn't afford pictures to hang on walls or decorations for their home. So, the Lewis family's environment failed to support the effervescent imaginations of two young boys. Lewis commented, "What the real garden had failed to do, the toy garden did."[37] Seeing the tiny garden on the biscuit tin gave Lewis an experience that set the stage for encounters with "joy" for the rest of his life. Listening to our tour guide tell that story sparked joy in our own hearts, helping us know Lewis better and savor joy deeply.

Lewis's experiences of joy took many forms—reading mythology, taking long walks, writing poetry, laughing with friends, listening to Wagner, and drinking tea. (He once told a friend, "You can't get a cup of tea large enough or a book long enough to suit me."[38]) Joy was everywhere. Correspondingly, after his conversion, it was easy for Lewis to see clues to the gospel everywhere—leading Walter Hooper, Lewis's secretary and close friend, to call him "the most thoroughly converted man I ever met."[39] All of life was now seen through the lens of the gospel, leading him to write, "I believe in Christianity as I believe that the Sun has risen, not only because I see it, but because by it I see everything else."[40]

When Lewis felt that pain of longing, he now knew where that ache would someday find complete healing. He realized that these unfulfilled desires were really pointers to another world—a world he knew he would reach because of the finished work of the cross. This way of seeing gave Lewis the evangelist a multitude of starting points to reach outsiders. These sparks of joy, he reasoned, were "clues" to something bigger.

## OLD TESTAMENT: CLUES IN THE TAPESTRY

You may be thinking, "This is all well and good. And I'm thankful C.S. Lewis had such an active imagination. But I'm not sure *I* see all that many connections between everyday life and the gospel." As always, the Bible can help us. The Scriptures are filled with clues that point us beyond them to the one who made a world "charged with the grandeur of God."[41] The Scriptures model and encourage a clue-based apologetic that is worth adding to our quiver of pre-evangelism strategies.

First, the Old Testament has a future orientation. Predictions and prophecies cause us to anticipate fulfillment. A pattern of "this points to that" seems to be woven in. Some events feel incomplete until a later ending brings finality. For example, in Genesis 22 Abraham, on God's command, offered up his son Isaac on a sacrificial altar—which points us to another son who was offered up by his father. God provided a ram to take Isaac's place, pointing us to Jesus' future role as the Lamb of God. The story is even told in a way that feels unfinished. Note the future tenses in Genesis 22 v 14-15: "Abraham called that place The LORD Will Provide. And to this day it is said, 'On the mountain of the LORD it will be provided.'" There was a future fulfillment of this amazing drama that was still to come.

Other Old Testament stories just seem odd, and that's why we wonder if we should keep reading to find a culmination or an explanation. When people rebelled against God and experienced his judgment through poisonous snakes, Moses fashioned a bronze snake and lifted it high on a pole so people could turn from their deadly situation, look up, and be saved (Numbers 21 v 4-9). If that story isn't a clue to a greater savior who was lifted high, it's just plain weird.

Second, the Old Testament has a symbolic feel to it. Physical things point to spiritual realities. "The heavens declare the glory of God," the psalmist tells us (Psalm 19 v 1). They're not just stars. They're the work of God's fingers (Psalm 8 v 3). As we read more and more of God's word, our eyes receive training to look beyond what is seen to what is unseen. "This points to that" becomes grander in scale.

Clues receive a fuller treatment in the book of Ecclesiastes— mostly in the form of disappointments. The Teacher, the book's author, explores work, wisdom, pleasure, building projects, beauty, riches, and other ventures, only to feel despair and emptiness. He wonders if all is meaningless. And yet, he also observes that "there is a time for everything, and a season for every activity under the heavens" (3 v 1). He concludes: "[God] has made everything beautiful in its time. He has also set eternity in the human heart" (3 v 11).

It's as if the Teacher can't allow himself to draw the totally empty conclusion of meaninglessness because he can't help seeing the clues that point in a different direction. He wrestles over this for hundreds of verses, falling repeatedly into the trap of looking "under the sun" for answers but ultimately (to the great relief of his readers!) concluding as follows:

*Fear God and keep his commandments, for this is the duty of all mankind. For God will bring every deed into judgment, including every hidden thing, whether it is good or evil. (Ecclesiastes 12 v 13-14)*

The crucial lesson from Ecclesiastes is this: keeping your perspective "under the sun" leads to meaninglessness. Lifting your eyes to God leads to contentment. Yet life "under the sun" is not unimportant. The Teacher also notes, "I know that there is nothing better for people than to be happy and to do good while they live. That each of them may eat and drink, and find satisfaction in all their toil—this is the gift of God" (Ecclesiastes 3 v 12-13).

C.S. Lewis helps us understand this theme by delineating "first and second things." The first things are the eternal ones—God's kingdom and knowing God as King. The second things are pretty much everything else. Lewis said, "You can't get second things by putting them first; you can get second things only by putting first things first."[42]

Yet we do put second things first. To some extent, everyone seeks satisfaction from things that cannot satisfy. Because God "has set eternity" in our hearts, we will pursue it. The tragedy is that we look for it in second things. We think the temporal can provide what only the eternal can.

When these temporal or second things disappoint, as they inevitably must, it can be crushing. But when people experience that disappointment, then the gospel can be heard as once long-lost but finally found good news. Second things can make us long for first things. This is why Lewis's sparks of joy serve as clues to the gospel.

## NEW TESTAMENT: CLUES IN THE HEART

A helpful example of using clues in evangelism comes in Acts 14, when Paul and Barnabas pointed some worshipers of Greek gods to the true God. They had healed a lame man, but the crowd did not attribute the healing power to God Almighty. Rather, "Barnabas they called Zeus, and Paul they called Hermes ... and [they] wanted to offer sacrifices to them" (Acts 14 v 12-13). Paul and Barnabas would have none of that and called the people to turn from their "worthless things." But then they pointed their hearers in a surprising direction. Rather than teaching from the Scriptures, as they had done in a Jewish synagogue (Acts 13 v 16-43), or quoting Greek poets, as they had done on Mars Hill (Acts 17 v 28), they talked about "rain from heaven and crops in their seasons ... plenty of food ... and hearts [filled] with joy" (Acts 14 v 17). It's as if Paul had asked them, "Where do you think all these good gifts come from?"

Don't miss that he affirmed that even they—unsaved people who worshiped false gods—could have joy in their hearts. I realize this may sound confusing because Paul used "joy" slightly differently than C.S. Lewis did. For Paul, joy is the experience of happiness that comes from the good things in life like food. For Lewis, it's the longing that's left after the food is gone. For our purposes, both fit together, as we try to show people how good things point to the best thing.

Paul's approach in Acts 14 is a joy-based apologetics, in contrast to a misery-based apologetics. Both work—but with different audiences.

Misery-based apologetics sounds like this: "Aren't you miserable trying to live your life apart from God? Don't you want more out of life than just possessions and experiences?" This is indeed how Jesus approached the woman at the well in John 4. But some people don't feel miserable apart from God—at least, not yet. Our appeals to their misery don't work because they're rather happy. For them, joy-based apologetics might work better: "Isn't it amazing how plants grow of their own accord and then we eat the fruit? Do you ever think about what a great gift that is?"

Both the pleasures provided by a good God and the disappointments of life apart from God can be clues that point people to God.

## MADE FOR ANOTHER WORLD

I've said that not everyone relates to this ache of longing. So this is not the evangelistic strategy for everyone. But I am convinced we should employ it more often than we do.

Recently, I sat in a crowded college cafeteria eating lunch by myself. I needed time alone (or so I thought) in between meetings where I taught or led. My hopes for recharging my introvert batteries were dashed when a man asked me, "Do you mind if I join you? There aren't any open tables in this whole food court." (Apparently God's estimation of my introversion doesn't match mine.) We struck up a conversation and found several points in common. We were both older than the undergraduate students all around us. I was part of a campus ministry staff. He was a retired man taking advantage of free courses offered to senior citizens. We both came from Jewish backgrounds and both enjoyed reading and lifelong learning.

When he heard about my faith, he asked, "How'd that happen?" I decided to share the part of my story that centers on hope and disappointment. I told him about my drunken days in high school and college and how they always left me empty. I told him I now think I was trying to find something that kept eluding me. Then I spoke about my love of music and all those concerts I attended. They too left me empty. I also admitted that Judaism—the way I practiced it—led to even greater frustration. I never felt that I could do enough to please God.

Next, I recounted my reading of C.S. Lewis's *Mere Christianity*. (My new friend told me he'd read all the *Narnia* series.) I spoke of how disappointments can lead to one of three conclusions. The first is endless pleasure seeking. The second is despairing cynicism.

At that point, he raised his hand as in a classroom. It was odd, but I called on him anyway. "That's me," he blurted out, loud enough to get stares from the surrounding tables. "I'm the cynic!"

"Me too!" I said, a bit more softly to reclaim the privacy of our conversation. Then I added, "C.S. Lewis offered a third option for handling the disappointments." He listened intently for the next ten minutes as I shared about being made for another world and how Jesus opened the door to that world.

Suddenly the man looked at his watch and saw he had to leave to go to his next class. He asked me the name of that book I had mentioned. "Did you say *Mirror Christianity*?" "Mere, not mirror," I said. He told me he would read it. I've prayed for him ever since.

Do you relate to this idea of joy as an unsatisfied desire? Can you remember moments when you wondered if you were made for another world? Was it through music? A story? An experience? A place? Try to bring those moments to the surface. It may help you connect others to the world they were made for.

This is more than a smooth intro to a gospel presentation. People who fail to realize they were made for another world set their affections on second things—and that's tragic. As Lewis observed, "The books or the music in which we thought the beauty was located will betray us if we trust to them; it was not *in* them, it only came *through* them, and what came through them was longing. These things—the beauty, the memory of our own past—are good images of what we really desire; but if they are mistaken for the thing itself, they turn into dumb idols, breaking the hearts of their worshippers."[43] When we share the gospel with people who have made second things into first things, we offer them liberation from having their hearts broken by their dumb idols.

We do need to acknowledge a weakness of this approach. Some have rightly critiqued Lewis's appeal to longing in evangelism because it downplays the seriousness of sin. Fair enough. When we offer clues that point to God, let's be sure to articulate what else we know about this God. He is holy and he judges sin. We long for him, but we also rebel against him.

Nevertheless, this approach does have an ironic advantage. Clues are not proofs. They don't pretend to completely settle the issue. They suggest more than insist. They ask someone to consider something rather than surrender to it. In so doing, clues may actually accomplish more by attempting less. When we tell people we have "proofs" for God's existence or Jesus' resurrection or the Bible's historicity, we may set ourselves up for pushback. Some people only need to find one loophole in a "proof" to justify their total rejection of it.

When I discussed *Mere Christianity* with a non-Christian friend, he showed me four pages of written objections. For example, when Lewis said that "selfishness has never been admired,"[44] my friend countered, "I can think of people who boast of their greed or cultures that do reward selfishness."

I despaired for a moment—then suggested, "True. But remember that Lewis was making general statements that are usually true. These were short radio broadcasts, after all. He wasn't trying to construct an elaborate philosophical treatise. Wouldn't you agree that most people think selfishness is bad? Don't most people try to be generous—and fail at it?" He agreed with me. Seeing Lewis's idea as a "clue" instead of a "proof" helped him get past his objections.

Regarding this approach, one of Lewis's closest friends, Austin Farrer, observed, "We think we are listening to an argument; in fact, we are presented with a vision; and it is the vision that carries conviction."[45]

## HOW TO LOOK FOR CLUES

Following Lewis's example means we can unlock conversations that might otherwise lead nowhere—or never happen at all. Here are three suggestions for how to use joy and longing to do just that.

First, observe where you already see "everything else" through the Christian lens. What parts of God's creation shine most vividly to you? Do you tend to see design on the beautiful/artistic end of the spectrum or on the scientific/factual end? When do you see something (or read or hear or learn or think something) and want to share it with someone else?

Explore *why* you find some things suggestive of more. What is it about seeing a huge tree or hearing a funny story or puzzling over a math problem that triggers a thought about God? Is it his power or his creativity or his splendor that draws you in? Develop moment by moment adoration for God's everyday gifts. This may broaden your scope of common ground with non-Christians you know. After saying something like "Isn't that sunset beautiful?" you might add, "Why do you suppose we're so captivated by beauty?" After enjoying a delicious meal with people of other faiths, perhaps a discussion about the God who provides such delicacies could follow.

Second, brainstorm starting points to connect people you know to the God you know. What common ground do you already share with friends? Sports? Politics? Gardening? Family? Golf? Where do these topics intersect with God's common grace? Sports might point people to the Creator who made the human body so marvelously. Politics might suggest God's design for us to live in harmony with others. Gardening could hint at a God who loves color and variety. Family invites us to appreciate intimacy and love. And golf—if you play like I do—shows the ugliness of sin and the horrors of hell!

Where do the people around you find joy in their hearts? How can you help them wonder where that joy comes from? A Christian friend of mine wanted to reach out to his neighbors. But he doubted they'd come to a Bible study. So he invited them to an evening of book sharing. Anyone could bring a favorite book and share why they liked it. Food and drinks made for a delightful evening and started many rich conversations. He did not share the gospel that night. But he has had many gospel conversations since. Their books served as clues to a grander story.

Finally, expand your palate for clues. Once you start looking, you can see evidence of another world in many places in this world. First think about the Bible's storyline and then search for clues that point toward it. For example:

- *Creation:* Beauty and order in physical creation are not hard to find. What clues in the natural world could help you point to God as Creator?
- *Fall:* Unfortunately, evidences of people's rebellion are also abundant. Many songs and movies express the darkness of the human heart.

- *Redemption:* Where can you find stories of a redeemer or deliverer? Try starting with superhero movies.
- *Consummation:* Cries for deliverance or longings for a new world can be seen far and wide with just a bit of reflection.

Engaging in joy-based, clue-filled conversations with your friends may help them see that their "lifelong nostalgia ... is no mere neurotic fancy, but the truest index of [their] real situation. And to be at last summoned inside would be both glory and honour beyond all [their] merits and also the healing of that old ache."[46]

# 3. THE HONORING OF
# OBJECTIONS

"Stop! ... What do you mean by wildness and what grounds had you for not expecting it?"[47] Such was the greeting C.S. Lewis received from his new tutor, W.T. Kirkpatrick, the very first time they met. Lewis was simply trying to make small talk: "I was surprised at the scenery of Surrey; it was much wilder than I had expected." That was all The Great Knock (as Lewis would always call him) needed to indeed knock his new pupil out from simplistic thinking about even the smallest of topics. Under Kirkpatrick's training, long before Lewis became a Christian, he sharpened the logic skills that would shape the rest of his life. Kirkpatrick, an atheist with no time for foolish religion, influenced Lewis in both thought and attitude far beyond what either could foresee.

When Lewis became a Christian, he applied those same skills and conditioning to thinking deeply about God, Jesus, faith, the Bible, and objections raised against the gospel. The Great Knock toughened him up for arguments about any and all subjects so he would never shy away from a disagreement. This explains why he targeted the most formidable argument against faith—*The Problem of Pain*—in his first published work of apologetics.

Even in the brief radio broadcasts that became *Mere Christianity*, Lewis dared to explore problems that many evangelists stay a million miles away from. In fact, some evangelism training programs explicitly dismiss intellectual questions as mere "smoke screens," which should be set aside as quickly as possible. Better to get on with the more important task of sharing the so-called "simple gospel," they insist. By contrast, Lewis's own conversion—coming as it did through rigorous intellectual debate—forged a deep respect for skeptics' intellectual questions. He never fell into the anti-intellectual trap that, unfortunately, many Christians fall into today.

In *Mere Christianity*, Lewis took on the difficult topics of the incarnation, the reality of the devil, the nature of evil, free will, the second coming, sex, and even Freudian psychology! He didn't opt to "keep it simple," because he knew that life is not simple—nor is belief in the Author of life. To be sure, we all need to know how to express our beliefs in clear, concise ways. But we mustn't confuse clear expression with shallow theology.

When Lewis began his fourth series of broadcasts, he complimented the intellects of his listeners and readers in this way: "Everyone has warned me not to tell you what I am going to tell you in this last book. They all say, 'the ordinary reader does not want Theology; give him plain practical religion'. I have rejected their advice. I do not think the ordinary reader is such a fool."[48]

Lewis knew what non-Christians thought and believed because he himself had thought and believed those very things not long before. He countered the popular notion that morality is just "herd instinct"—something different societies formulate differently—by highlighting examples of universally held ethics.[49] He unraveled the theory that New Testament stories were mere fables by comparing them to works of fiction, a collection he knew well. He articulated and then dismantled the common notion that Jesus was a mere man or just a very good teacher by listing the many extreme claims he made. One by one, he articulated common obstacles to belief even better than skeptics did; he took them seriously and carefully removed them. We need to develop that same flow in our evangelism.

## RESPECTING THE QUESTIONER

What may not seem immediately evident from reading Lewis's apologetic works is his respect for the questions and the questioners. We might misread his answers as dismissive disregard of them because he was so clear and concise. But that would be a terrible mistake. Don't equate brevity with dismissal. The very fact that Lewis spent so much time and energy in public evangelism and written apologetics should show us that he cared deeply about reaching lost people. He presented evangelistic talks at military bases as well as academic gatherings and wrote numerous letters to skeptics, sharing about his own conversion through logical debate and working hard at making answers accessible and understandable to all. "If you cannot translate your thoughts into uneducated language," he instructed would-be apologists, "then your thoughts were confused. Power to translate is the test of having really understood one's own meaning."[50]

When actress Debra Winger read some of Lewis's works in preparing to play Joy Davidman in the movie *Shadowlands*, she remarked, "He [makes] difficult questions accessible. I don't think he makes the answers 'easy'. I don't think he answers questions. I think he discusses them. He's in that school of discourse where his statements are not like books that are written by experts. He's saying, 'think about this'. That's why I think he opened Christianity to so many people."[51]

Lewis may not have supported his perspective from the book of Proverbs, but we can shape our handling of objections that way. Proverbs 16 v 25 says, "There is a way that appears to be right, but in the end it leads to death." If something people believe appears to be right to them, we should ask why. We can develop compassion for people by wondering what draws them to certain beliefs, no matter how wrong they may seem to us. We need to listen in order to understand and appreciate, rather than only to respond or refute.

Some may worry that this kind of empathy can lead to relativism on our part. But there is little danger of adopting ideas like "there is no right or wrong" or "all truths lead to same place" if we balance compassion with truth. In fact, careful listening can clarify (in our thinking and in our sharing) the differences between truth and error. As Lewis put it, "If you are a Christian, you are free to think that all those religions, even the queerest ones, contain at least some hint of the truth … But, of course, being a Christian does mean thinking that where Christianity differs from other religions, Christianity is right and they are wrong."[52]

## MAKING THE CHALLENGE

Lewis helps us most through his models for challenging objections. Often, he first weakens objections before offering alternatives. He parries an argument against the gospel by seamlessly turning it into a support for the gospel. For example, responding to the objection that Christians accept Jesus' authority blindly, he countered, "Do not be scared by the word authority. Believing things on authority only means believing them because you have been told them by someone you think trustworthy. Ninety-nine per cent of the things you believe are believed on authority."[53]

Again, in one of his many discussions of the problem of evil, he said, "My argument against God was that the universe seemed so cruel and unjust. But how had I got this idea of just and unjust? A man does not call a line crooked unless he has some idea of a straight line."[54] He was pointing out the hole in the logic. Or again, on the same topic, countering the improbability that people merely invented the notion of a good god, he wondered why "the great religions were first preached, and long practised, in a world without [the anesthetic] chloroform."[55] If ever there was a time when people would not think God was good, it was when they faced levels of pain and suffering that we moderns can't even imagine. But some of the loftiest praises of God's goodness were penned from places of discomfort and struggle. Putting his opponents on the defensive, Lewis said, "Christianity ... is a religion you could not have guessed."[56]

Against the position that the gospels were myths or fiction, he played his card as literature scholar: "I've read a great many novels and I know a fair amount about the legends that grew up among early people, and I know perfectly well the Gospels are not that kind of stuff. They're absolutely full of the sort of things that don't come into legends."[57]

The Great Knock would have been proud of his quick identification of arguments as self-refuting. One of Lewis's correspondents remembered, "As a graduate student at Columbia, I began to question the validity of reason ... I wrote to Lewis about my misgivings. His reply was the shortest letter I received from him—two sentences: "Your letter finds me in the midst of exams and a complete reply is impossible now. If you are losing your faith in reason, why did you use all those reasons to tell me so?"[58]

Did you notice the power of asking a question as a challenge? What effect do you think his question had on the person who doubted reason? What do questions do that statements don't? Have you noticed that I keep asking questions?[59]

## THE BIBLE'S APOLOGETIC FOR APOLOGETICS

Honoring objections flows out of honoring people. Every questioner bears the image of God: a marred image, to be sure, but that does not negate the need to treat all people with dignity and respect. Remember Peter's admonition to "always be prepared to give an answer to everyone who asks you to give the reason for the hope that you have. But do this with gentleness and respect" (1 Peter 3 v 15). Note the extent of the command. Always. Everyone. And consider that Peter's words came during a time of great persecution. Don't overlook the insertion of "but" before the qualities of gentleness and respect. Apparently, it's easy to give answers without gentleness or respect—especially during times of hostility toward the gospel.

I recently found myself stuck in traffic behind a car with a lot of bumper stickers. Most were variations of the "Coexist" slogan, in which the letters in the word "coexist" are replaced by symbols of various religions. The message was reinforced by other stickers that exhorted readers to respect "all points of view." One sticker caused me to laugh. It read, "Coexist: Even with the Jerks." I wondered how to reconcile the terms "respect" and "jerks." Sometimes the plea for "tolerance" can be remarkably intolerant. And that is the climate into which we are called to be ready to offer answers to everyone who asks—even the jerks!

Fortunately, we have a resource for extending gentleness and respect to people who might not reciprocate. And it's better than hundreds of bumper stickers. We have the gentleness and respect of God our Savior extended to us through his atoning death on the cross. If we're tempted to treat people harshly because they raise their objections in unkind ways, we can recall how we ourselves have treated God in unkind, even blasphemous ways. We, undeserving rebels, have been brought near. We, apathetic sinners, have been adopted. Before Peter gives us the command to give answers to outsiders, he reminds us that we "have been chosen according to the foreknowledge of God the Father, through the sanctifying work of the Spirit, to be obedient to Jesus Christ" (1 Peter 1 v 2). Allowing that truth to wash over us prepares us to "always be prepared ... with gentleness and respect."

Occasionally, people challenge this notion of preparing answers or constructing defenses ahead of time. "Doesn't Jesus tell us not to worry about what to say or how to say it?" they ask. They're referring to Matthew 10 v 19, where Jesus does indeed say that. He even adds, "At that time you will be given what to say, for it will not be you speaking, but the Spirit of your Father speaking through you." But notice the context. That promise comes to those who are being arrested and "brought before governors and kings" (Matthew 10 v 18). It's for handling a trial in court, not a conversation over coffee. Peter's call to prepare still stands for our evangelistic efforts.

## A TEST CASE

Let's apply these apologetic principles to one example: the common objection of exclusivity.[60]

We begin by anticipating the objection. Many non-Christians object strongly to the "intolerant" view that Jesus is the only way to eternal life. What could be more arrogant, they argue, than insisting on having the only truth? In fact, some even accuse us of having unchristian (that is, uncharitable) beliefs and attitudes toward others by insisting that everyone needs to agree with us. Given the high esteem for diversity in our culture currently, we must anticipate this question and prepare helpful responses.

Next, we need to respect the question by understanding it better and empathizing with it more deeply. As recently as the middle of the twentieth century, our world didn't seem quite so diverse. People of other religions lived far away from us. For most people in the West, diversity meant "Protestant, Catholic, and Jew."[61] Muslims, Buddhists, Hindus, and people of other faiths were on the other side of the planet. And we only knew about atheists from philosophy classes. Today, by contrast, religious diversity is evident on every street, in every classroom, and at every work station. Most everyone knows people with radically different beliefs and, when we get to know them, we find that these people don't seem so bad. Certainly, they don't strike us as people destined for eternal separation from a loving God. Not only that, but their views likely stem from a rich cultural heritage which we're wary of dismissing.

That's how many people feel when they ask a question or make an accusation about exclusivity. We can only answer people "with gentleness and respect" if we take the time to feel what they feel.

So, then, how do we argue for "Jesus is the only way" in a world that values so many different ways? We must do so by first challenging the question itself. Just as Lewis did many times, we need to turn the burden of defense onto the questioner before offering a better way of thinking about the issue.

We can start by pointing out the intolerance woven into the question, "How can you say yours is the only way?" This takes time but, eventually, we need to say and we need to help our friends see that everyone is exclusive. Every worldview is intolerant. When people say, "You should never tell anyone that their religion is wrong," they are telling us that our religion is wrong. If they boast, "I would never condemn anyone's religion," they just condemned our religion. The idea that all religions lead to the same place is a relatively recent, post-Enlightenment point of view that belittles what the vast majority of religious people have believed for centuries. In criticizing what they see as self-righteousness, the skeptic has displayed their own form of self-righteousness.

Again, I must warn you, it is not easy to help people see the inconsistency behind their apparent "open-mindedness." But in most conversations, we must first level the playing field before presenting our perspective. Until our skeptical friends see their own haughtiness, our arguments may fall on deaf ears.

To do this with gentleness and respect, try using questions to tease out what your friend really thinks. Asking a question softens the argument, making it easier to accept. Or start by using an example that has nothing to do with them, so that it can't seem like a personal attack.

Our next phase of challenging the question could sound like this: "You've said that Christianity is only one way to God. But if there are many ways, it would seem to me that the Christian way is rather cruel. If people could get to God by believing the doctrines of other religions, isn't it horrible that God killed Jesus for some people's sins?"[62] In some ways, this echoes the argument Paul made in Galatians 2 v 21: "If righteousness could be gained through the law, Christ died for nothing." In other words, our conversation partner, who condemns condemnation, has just condemned Christianity.

Once we have challenged our challenger's beliefs, we can offer the gospel as something better. All religions are exclusive—but what if there was one kind of exclusivity that was the most inclusive? What if one exclusive faith was offered to anyone, regardless of their worthiness or performance? Might there be an exclusive belief system that "lead[s] their believers to be the most loving and receptive to those with whom they differ?"[63]

## BEING PREPARED

Getting ready to respond to objections may seem overwhelming. But it works well to break the task down into smaller steps.

First, it's helpful to examine our own abilities to respond to objections. Has there been someone in your life who has shaped you the way The Great Knock shaped Lewis? Perhaps your training for your profession has made you a more logical thinker or a more skeptical inquirer—or more curious to learn, or more able to see connections between things that other people only see as separate.

Or perhaps God's call on your life involves more practical tasks than academic ideas. Perhaps you serve people in very tangible ways. How have your experiences shaped your compassion for people or your capacity to show care? How have years (or decades!) of accomplishing physical tasks or fixing broken things expanded your patience or common sense? Your job, if you have one, is not just a vehicle for making money. Your vocation (a much better word than job) has shaped you in ways you may not have examined or appreciated.

Based on all of this, think about what kind of discussion you'd be best placed to have. What common objections do you feel most confident to challenge? What settings do you think you could most easily challenge them in? Ask God to allow these God-ordained strengths of yours to connect with God-implanted longings in your friends.

Next, it is worth taking another look at the list of non-Christians you pray for. What objections are they likely to raise? Are they questions about suffering? Exclusivity? The Bible? Morality? Hypocrisy? Something else? Have they raised some of these objections already? How have you handled them in the past? It's easy to get overwhelmed by trying to tackle all of them at once. Pick one and try to find answers online or in good apologetics books. Think of one or two statements you can make as *part* of an answer. Start the conversation there and take one step at a time. Prepare for more of a long hike than a short stroll.

What about those friends who never ask questions about faith or God or religion? That may account for most (or all!) of the people on your prayer list—but don't assume there's no drama going on inside their heads. You may be surprised how they'll respond if you wonder out loud with something like "You know I'm interested in spiritual things, right? Do you ever wonder about those kinds of topics?" or "If you don't want to talk about this, that's ok. But I'm curious about your spiritual beliefs. Have you ever been interested in faith or things like that?" Invite them to air their objections by asking what stops them from investigating faith more—or even start by wondering aloud what they think holds people back from belief *in general*.

Here's another idea. Don't be afraid to restart dialogues. You may feel you missed an opportunity when someone asked you a question. Perhaps you did! But asking for a second chance does not hurt. In fact, it could communicate to your friend that you care about them enough to mull over their question. It might also display a kind of humility that they rarely see in Christians. Returning to a previously blown opportunity could sound like this: "Do you remember that time you asked me that question about God and I didn't know how to answer? I've been thinking about it. I think it's a really important question. Would you be up for discussing it again? I still don't have all the answers, but I'd love to talk to you about it."

One final caution: I do not think this process of responding to strongly held objections is easy. Neither did C.S. Lewis. He warned, "This is very troublesome and it means you can say very little in half an hour, but it is essential."[64] When we read through the book of Acts, we don't get the sense that spreading the gospel has ever been easy: Peter, Paul, and other early believers racked up an impressive catalog of imprisonments, beatings, and straightforward rejection. But, in addition to presenting the most important message we could offer, honoring people's objections can be one of the greatest expressions of love we can extend. It also helps to remember how this rigorous process might end: "There is rejoicing in the presence of the angels of God over one sinner who repents" (Luke 15 v 10). Remembering this will help us as we endeavor to keep meeting our challengers with gentleness, respect, and honor.

# 4. THE STIRRING OF

# UNEASINESS

God has blessed my wife and me with three sons. We chose to give them biblical names—Daniel, David, and Jonathan. We considered other Old Testament names as well. But not for a second did we entertain the name that Isaiah gave his firstborn: Shear-Jashub (see Isaiah 7 v 3). What would his friends call him? He'd be laughed out of the playground.

Though not suitable for a name today, "Shear-Jashub" must be understood if we are to grasp a major theme of the Bible. The name means "a remnant will return," and it mirrors the ultimate good-news-bad-news message of the Bible—God is both a holy Judge and a gracious Redeemer. Isaiah had been warning Israel that if they didn't turn back to God, he would force them out of the land he had given them. As part of his prophecy, Isaiah named his sons as "signs and symbols" (see Isaiah 8 v 18) to show just how seriously God intended to carry out his plan. The stiff-necked people did not listen, and God carried out what he had foretold.

There are both good-news and bad-news components of "a remnant will return." The good news for Israel is: you won't stay cast out of the land forever. The bad news is: you *will* be cast out! Israel had been in the land, enjoying its plenty and their freedom, when Isaiah's son was born and named.

But they would not remain there. Only a remnant (not all) would return. That's even more bad news.

God will judge severely. But he will also forgive graciously. What does this have to do with C.S. Lewis's approach to evangelism and how we can follow his lead? Simply this: people need to hear both the good news and the bad news in our message. They need to sense there's a problem before they open up to a solution—to feel tension before they long for resolution. Salvation comes to those who wonder how God can be both holy and loving, a law-giver and a sin-forgiver, a judge and a savior. To use Lewis's language, we all must admit that "we have cause to be uneasy."[65]

## THE TENSION IN SCRIPTURE

God has woven these parallel themes of judgment and forgiveness throughout the Old Testament, surfacing a tension that only gets resolved in the New Testament. Let's explore that first—then we'll consider how C.S. Lewis used this tension in his outreach and how we can do the same.

We already saw in chapter 2 how some Old Testament stories seem unfinished. God has also woven another thread into his Old Testament tapestry—the theme of unresolved tension. In many places, we read of God's holiness and his grace, and are forced to wonder, "How can both of these be true?"

For example, in the dramatic scene in Exodus 34, after Moses asked to see God's glory and God promised to allow his goodness to pass in front of him, God declared, "The Lord, the Lord, the compassionate and gracious God, slow to anger, abounding in love and faithfulness, maintaining love to thousands, and forgiving wickedness, rebellion and sin" (Exodus 34 v 6-7). We'd like the passage to end there. But it doesn't. God continues, "Yet he does not leave the guilty unpunished; he punishes the children and their children for the sin of the parents to the third and fourth generation." God is so loving that he forgives sin. But he's so holy that he punishes sin. Do you feel the tension? This text does not resolve it, nor does it even hint at how that resolution may someday come. This passage gets quoted or alluded to in many other passages that follow—in Numbers, Nehemiah, the Psalms, and by the prophets Joel, Jonah, and Nahum.[66] You could say this is a dominant melody in God's symphony.

Once we recognize this unresolved tension, we start seeing it in many places throughout God's word. For another example, consider Psalm 98. This is a beautiful two-part call to praise God, for "he has done marvelous things" (v 1). The first part (v 1-3) tells of God's love and salvation. The second part (v 4-9) tells of his judgment and equity. Both sections say these attributes express God's righteousness (v 2 and 9). It is indeed right for God to be a God of love. And it is also right for him to judge with equity. But the psalm does not explain how both can be true. If God loves us, wouldn't he forgive us? If he forgives us, doesn't that compromise his justice?

Occasionally, God sneaks in hints or foreshadowings of a way in which the tension will get resolved. They are often cryptic and difficult to interpret. Their very oddness highlights the need to pay close attention to them. For centuries, Jewish scholars have identified these texts as Messianic.[67] Careful readers of the Scriptures longed for a deliverer who had been promised numerous times in various ways.

The very first mention of a resolution of tension comes immediately after the rebellion in the Garden of Eden. God promised one who would crush the serpent's head, foreseeing a conflict that would bring about a righting of the wrong in the garden. Poetic predictions can be seen in Psalms 16 and 22. The specifics of a "faithful one" not seeing decay (16 v 10) or a despised and scorned sufferer who has his hands and feet pierced (22 v 16) are too far-reaching to find their fulfillment in David or any other mere human. The most elaborate prediction—of one who would suffer as a means of atonement to resolve the tension of God's righteous judgment and his unfailing love—comes in Isaiah 53. Here we find the previously mentioned sufferings to have a purpose: "By his wounds we are healed" (Isaiah 53 v 5). The coming Messiah would resolve the greatest tension with the most remarkable resolution—by taking the judgment for sin upon himself to allow sinners to be forgiven.

Much more could be said about the prominent Old Testament theme of a prophesied Messiah.[68] For our purposes, suffice it to say, a deep appreciation for the ways in which Jesus' death satisfies God's holiness and his love can be a deep reservoir from which to evangelize. When we marvel that God is both "just and the one who justifies" (Romans 3 v 26), we can offer people the solution they long for after they accept that they have "cause to be uneasy."

## DELIVERING THE BAD NEWS

Some have explained the hypocrisy of Western culture by calling it a "cut-flower culture." When we buy a bouquet of flowers, they are cut off from their roots. We bring them home and put them in water and enjoy their beauty—but only for a short time. Sooner or later, because of their lack of rootedness in a source of nutrients and life, they die. In fact, the dying process begins as soon as the flower is cut. But for a time, they still appear vibrant and alive. Such is the case in our culture when it comes to morality and sin. We have cut ourselves off from biblical roots that support morality, but we still want (to some extent) the fruit of that morality. We hear it most painfully when people who have separated sex from marriage lament that their current bed partner cheated on them.

Lewis saw the beginnings of modern secular culture and labeled it as a "tragi-comedy" in which "we continue to clamour for those very qualities we are rendering impossible."[69] For example, most of our educational institutions repeat the mantras "there is no right or wrong" and "there are no absolutes," but still insist on grading papers and exams using a standard of right and wrong. Or we tell people that everyone creates their own morality, but then we criticize them for not holding to a high moral standard. Lewis said it best: "In a sort of ghastly simplicity we remove the organ and demand the function. We make men without chests and expect of them virtue and enterprise. We laugh at honour and are shocked to find traitors in our midst. We castrate and bid the geldings be fruitful."[70]

Pointing out this "cut-flower syndrome" is one way of surfacing the bad-news-good-news tension. Good news: a trustworthy moral framework does exist. Bad news: you're not following it. The tension which lies both in our society's double standards and in its continual reinterpretation of moral rules makes both the good news and bad news evident.

The great challenge is to point out that tension with gentleness and respect, not self-righteousness and sarcasm. We want people to feel uneasy, yes; but we also want them to keep listening.

C.S. Lewis is a model in how to do this. Many people have found themselves laughing out loud while reading Lewis, only to have that laughter come to an abrupt halt when the joke turns on them. He was a genius at pointing out hypocrisy—in theory and in lives, especially his own. This disarmed opponents. Lewis was not afraid to deliver the bad news that humans are sinful and deserve judgment, but he did so in a way that made his readers and conversation partners recognize that, deep down, they already suspected that this was true. This moved them gently toward the repentance that leads to salvation.

Lewis would have been proud of one undergraduate student I knew. She listened intently as one of her professors spoke at length about how there are no absolutes, how everyone determines their own reality, and how words only mean what the hearer wants them to mean. "We need to mourn the death of the author," he told the class, insisting that "authorial intent" should be abandoned just as we gave up the belief in a flat earth. My acquaintance raised her hand and asked if that same interpretive method should be applied to the course syllabus. She asked, "When we read, 'The final paper is due on April 3rd,' may we ascribe the meaning, 'The final paper is never due'?"

In some conversations with thoughtful non-Christians we can follow Lewis's lead to show how some arguments contradict themselves. Not everyone will want to take the discussion to this level. But, for some, this is absolutely crucial.

For example, many non-Christians value science. (We should agree with them, by the way). But some take it to a belief in scientism: a view that observable, provable "facts" are the *only* way to know anything. The problem is, that view is not itself scientifically provable. It's an article of faith. As Lewis put it, "When I accept Theology I may find difficulties … but I can get in, or allow for, science as a whole … I can understand how men should come, by observation and inference, to know a lot about the universe they live in. If, on the other hand, I swallow the scientific cosmology as a whole, then not only can I not fit in Christianity, but I cannot even fit in science."[71] After all, if you can only know what you can touch, how can you trust the processes of thought, reasoning, and deduction that happen inside your own head?

Lewis penetrated further when he left aside theoretical questions and pointed his comments more personally. Stated most simply, he argued that people "ought to behave in a certain way" and "they do not in fact behave in that way."[72] For example, we all know people who annoy us or have glaring faults and are blind to them. We insist these people need to change, but no one can seem to get through to them. Anyone will recognize this scenario. But then Lewis would have us consider the situation from God's point of view. "[God] sees one more person of the same kind—the one you never do see. I mean, of course, yourself. That is the next great step in wisdom—to realise that you also are just that sort of person."[73] We find ourselves caught in the very snare we were willing to lay for someone else.

There is evangelistic power in sharing our own hypocrisy or inconsistency when dialoguing with outsiders. Honestly admitting our own sin can help others do the same. For example, Lewis wrote, "I remember Christian teachers telling me long ago that I must ... hate the sin but not the sinner. For a long time I used to think this a silly, straw-splitting distinction: how could you hate what a man did and not hate the man? But years later it occurred to me that there was one man to whom I had been doing this all my life—namely myself."[74]

## A TERRIBLE FIX

The gospel is the best news we can share with people. But it's also the worst. They have to acknowledge the bad news before they'll accept the good news. Our task is to "open wounds and heal them with the Gospel" as Lewis did.[75] Only then will they appreciate Jesus' death as the best and the worst news they could ever hear. This resonates with what Tolkien called the "eucatastrophe" (that is, a very good solution brought about by something that, at first, seemed very bad).

The Bible's tension resonates with people's internal tension. In the Bible, it's the tension between God's holiness and his love. In us, it's the tension between our demand for righteousness and our lack of attaining it. (Of course, people don't necessarily call it righteousness. They say, "That's not fair," or "That's not right" or "Nobody should do that" or countless other "shoulds.") When people see the problem in the Scriptures and recognize it in themselves, they take crucial steps toward salvation.

But please note: we need patience and gentleness in the way we help them cross the threshold of faith. It takes patience because the process may not go as quickly as we'd like. It takes gentleness because the experience of rebirth, like physical birth, may be painful. It has similarities to what Job felt when, confronted by God's holiness and his own unworthiness, he put his hand over his mouth (Job 40 v 4).

Some have found it helpful to point out the bad-news part of the gospel by preaching law before grace. They hold up rules and show how we break them.

The tactic of preaching law before grace looks to the Sermon on the Mount (especially Matthew 5 v 21-30) as a guide. For example, Jesus elicited agreement from his hearers that murder is wrong. Then he showed how condemning people with words stems from the same source as murder. He did the same with adultery and lust. An honest hearer would have to respond with "Woe is me." Only then will the offer of forgiveness, through a substitute's atonement, find a receptive heart.

This tactic works well in some situations but not all. Of course, that can be said about any and all approaches to evangelism. But I would offer a caution in employing this law-before-grace strategy. It can sound heavy-handed and push people away from the gospel. Some will feel berated or backed into a corner if the interrogation goes like this: "Have you ever lied? What does that make you? A liar, right? Do you know what God says about lying?" Far better to change the pronouns from "you" to "we." "We all want people to be truthful with us, right? But don't we sometimes deceive them? We use phrases like 'tell a little white lie' or 'stretch the truth,' but it's lying, isn't it? We hold people to a standard that we can't keep, don't we?"

As Lewis put it, "We know that if there does exist an absolute goodness it must hate most of what we do. This is the terrible fix we are in ... God is the only comfort, he is also the supreme terror: the thing we most need and the thing we most want to hide from."[76] When people admit this terrible fix, we can then tell them about the God who plants the standard of perfection in us and forgives us when we fail to keep that standard. He demands payment for sin, but he also provides payment for sin.

## SURFACING THE TENSION

Let's brainstorm some possible tension-raising questions or comments to steer conversations in gospel directions. You might want to do this together with friends—perhaps a church community group or Bible study. If I were in your group, here are some ideas I might suggest:

- "Isn't it amazing how we have both good and bad inside us?"
- "Do you ever wonder why we can be so nice one minute and so mean the next?"
- "Sometimes the world amazes me. We can see such wonderful beauty and horrible ugliness side by side. Do you know what I mean?"
- "Stories in the news can drive you crazy, can't they? One story tells of how people do such sacrificial things for each other. And the next story is all about cruelty. Do you ever wonder about that?"
- "I saw this great movie the other day. But it got me thinking about how life can seem so meaningful one minute and so pointless the next. Have you seen it? Would you be up for talking about it?"

Start looking for these kinds of tensions or juxtapositions in the world around you. They may be more plentiful than you've ever noticed. Start pointing them out to other people.

They may be wondering how to resolve tensions and you might be the one to help them.

Years ago, my wife and I were relaxing around our dining-room table after enjoying a delicious meal when, suddenly, we smelled a terrible odor of something burning. We both jumped up and ran to the kitchen, where we thought something must have caught on fire. But we couldn't find the source of the smell. We decided to do a thorough cleaning of the kitchen and dining room to get rid of the problem.

The next night, thirty minutes after we sat down to dinner, that same smell returned. Again, we searched. Again, we found nothing. The third night, we relived the same sequence—no odor/delicious dinner/relaxing conversation/horrible odor returns. This time, as we searched around the dining room, I noticed a blown-out lightbulb in the lamp above our dining room table. When I stood on a chair to replace the bulb, I smelled the source of the problem. The very old lamp had ceramic sockets that, over time, had deteriorated. After thirty minutes of warming up, it emitted that horrible odor. The source of the smell had been found!

This was bad news. I was going to have buy a new lamp (that costs money!) and install it (that means work!). Two doses of bad news in one sniff. But, in this case, learning bad news led to good news. Salvation came in the form of a new lamp and a few hours of work. But I never would have experienced the good news had I not discovered the bad news. Many of our gospel conversations need to follow that same sequence.

Up until this point, we have mostly examined pre-evangelism—things we say or do that raise the likelihood of a response to evangelism. In the chapters that follow, we'll turn more toward evangelism—proclaiming and clarifying the good news. We needed to spend this much time on pre-evangelism for, as Lewis argued, "Christianity simply does not make sense until you have faced the sort of facts I have been describing. Christianity tells people to repent and promises them forgiveness. It therefore has nothing (as far as I know) to say to people who do not know they have done anything to repent of and who do not feel that they need any forgiveness … Christian religion … does not begin in comfort; it begins in the dismay I have been describing, and it is no use at all trying to go on to that comfort without first going through that dismay."[77]

Where do you see those tensions in your own journey of faith? Can you identify them in other people's lives? Do you see ways in which people long for goodness or rightness or purity and can't attain it? Where do you see evidence of our "cut-flower" culture?

If some of your conversations end with the non-Christian feeling dismay, you've done good work. The task remains unfinished. But you're moving in the right direction. In fact, you both are.

# 5. THE CENTRALITY OF THE GOSPEL

Years ago, I attended an evangelism training seminar where our instructor painted this scenario: "Suppose you were standing on a street corner and you saw a man get hit by a car—right in front of you. It was obvious that he was about to die and there was no way to save him. You had only one minute to tell him the gospel. What would you say?"

Hands flew in the air as people eagerly shared what they'd say to this dying man. "Believe on the Lord Jesus Christ and you shall be saved!" "Turn or burn!" "Do you know Jesus as your personal Lord and Savior?"

I just sat there paralyzed. It all seemed so upsetting. I wanted to yell, "The man is dying. Aren't you horrified?" I couldn't get past the extremity of the hypothetical scene. I've been puzzled ever since. I really don't know what I'd say. The best I've come up with is "Stay calm. I'll call for an ambulance."

The seminar did convince me, however, that I was not prepared to articulate the gospel clearly and concisely—in any situation, let alone something as dire as a car accident.

## GETTING TO THE POINT

If, as I argued in chapter 1, the Old Testament is preparatory, then the New Testament is arrival. It presents itself as the goal to which all the previous material pointed. Indeed, Paul says that "Christ is the culmination of the law" (Romans 10 v 4). If the Old Testament feels like a building of anticipation and the asking of questions, the New Testament feels like "Ahhhhh. Relief!" and "The answer I've been waiting for."

It should come as no surprise that I think our evangelism should follow the same pattern. Even with all I've said so far about the importance of pre-evangelism and how C.S. Lewis mastered that tactic, there comes a time when all the preparation is done. The time has come for a clear, concise, and compelling presentation of the good news.

In the Scriptures, it all centers on the radical claims Jesus made about himself. He claimed to be one with the Father, a claim of deity (John 10 v 30-31). He said he was alive before the creation of the world, when "Satan [fell] like lightning from heaven" (Luke 10 v 18)—a bizarre delusion of grandeur if that's not the truth. And he said he'd still be with his disciples "always, to the very end of the age" (Matthew 28 v 20).

To the many people who have been indoctrinated (as I was) to think that Jesus was just a good teacher, the Gospels can seem like a splash of cold water in the face. Many of those who met Jesus in the flesh felt the same way. Let's look more closely at just two of these interactions.

One time, Jesus baffled religious leaders with this: "Abraham rejoiced at the thought of seeing my day; he saw it and was glad" (John 8 v 56). Then, adding the boldest of exclamation points, he said, "Before Abraham was born, I AM!" (v 58, my emphasis). He wasn't just saying he's always existed (a rather astonishing claim); he was invoking the name of God—I AM—which the Jewish tradition forbade anyone from uttering. The leaders understood his claim to deity. That's why they picked up stones to kill him.

On another occasion, the crowd charged Jesus with the same crime when he forgave the sins of the man who was paralyzed. They remarked, "Why does this fellow talk like that? He's blaspheming! Who can forgive sins but God alone?" (Mark 2 v 7) Who indeed?! It's one thing, if you step on my foot and I say, "I forgive you." But it's bizarre, if you step on somebody else's foot and I tell you, "I forgive you." You might reply, "Who are you to forgive me for stepping on someone else's foot? Mind your own business!" When Jesus forgave the sins of the paralyzed man, he was claiming the man had sinned against God and that he, Jesus, was the offended party—God! It is not hard to understand the outrage of the teachers of the law.

Jesus' proclamation of himself was truly bold. Sometimes we should just quote these claims and allow their extremity to do the heavy evangelistic lifting for us.

## LEWIS'S GOSPEL BOLDNESS

When historian George Marsden wrote his "biography" of C.S. Lewis's *Mere Christianity*, he concluded, "The lasting appeal of *Mere Christianity* is based on the luminosity of the Gospel message itself."[78] Lewis would have approved of his word choice: luminosity—the intrinsic brightness of an object. He helped countless readers and listeners see the brightness of the gospel by stating it as boldly as Jesus did.

Lewis realized that many people in his culture had heard clichés or vague statements of the Christian faith that lulled them into a non-thinking stupor. If that was true in his day, it seems far more prevalent in ours. Lewis chose to wake people up, as if to say, "Do you hear that? Isn't that preposterous? But maybe it's true!" In *Mere Christianity*, after more than fifty pages of preparation, Lewis boldly wrote, "Then comes the real shock. Among these Jews there suddenly turns up a man who goes about talking as if He was God. He claims to forgive sins. He says He has always existed. He says He is coming to judge the world at the end of time ... what this man said was, quite simply, the most shocking thing that has ever been uttered by human lips."[79]

Catch the clarity and the bluntness here: "We are told that Christ was killed for us, that His death has washed out our sins, and that by dying He disabled death itself. That is the formula. That is Christianity. That is what has to be believed."[80] No wonder he concluded, "Christianity is a statement which, if false, is of *no* importance, and, if true, of infinite importance. The one thing it cannot be is moderately important."[81]

Lewis wove bold proclamation with remarkably clear explanation. To clarify the difficult concepts of atonement and repentance, Lewis put it this way: "Only a bad person needs to repent. Only a good person can repent perfectly. The worse you are the more you need it and the less you can do it. The only person who could do it perfectly would be a perfect person— and he would not need it."[82] Following the pattern of the New Testament's relief after the Old Testament's anticipation, he wrote, "But supposing God became a man—suppose our human nature which can suffer and die was amalgamated with God's nature in one person—then that person could help us. He could surrender His will, and suffer and die, because He was man; and He could do it perfectly because He was God."[83]

Another tool Lewis used was to starkly contrast the gospel with alternatives. Sometimes he compared Jesus with other religious leaders so as to eliminate the claim that he was just like them: "If you had gone to Buddha and asked him, 'Are you the son of Brahmah?' he would have said, 'My son, you are still in the vale of illusion.' If you had gone to Socrates and asked, 'Are you Zeus?' he would have laughed at you. If you had gone to Mohammed and asked, 'Are you Allah?' he would first have rent his clothes and then cut your head off. If you had asked Confucius, 'Are you Heaven?' I think he would have probably replied, 'Remakes which are not in accordance with nature are in bad taste.'"[84]

Similarly, Lewis also compared Christianity as a whole to other belief systems. Boldly, he said atheism is "too simple," because reality is complex. He loved to compare the true gospel to what he called "Christianity and water" or "Soft soap" or a vague "Life-Force." He meant the kinds of religion that claim to be Christian without belief in the supernatural or the miraculous. (This kind of theologically liberal Christianity was prevalent in his day and hasn't disappeared in ours. So we would do well to show people the contrast between the true gospel and its liberal alternatives.) At the end of just his fourth radio broadcast, Lewis left his listeners with this to ponder for a full week: "The Life-Force is a sort of tame God. You can switch it on when you want, but it will not bother you. All the thrills of religion and none of the cost. Is the Life-Force the greatest achievement of wishful thinking the world has yet seen?"[85]

Preparing ourselves to disagree with people, contrasting our beliefs with theirs, may be one of the most important evangelistic skills we can develop. We should add the following kinds of prepared comments to our quiver of evangelistic arrows:

- "I know a lot of people believe that Jesus was just a good teacher. I think his words rule that out."
- "Some people think Christianity is just being nice to people. That misses the most important part."
- "You've said that Christianity is basically the same as all the other religions. I disagree. Can I tell you why?"

But perhaps we are getting ahead of ourselves here. Addressing our friends' incorrect assumptions is a good way of moving a conversation on to an explanation of the gospel. But we also need to be prepared to make that explanation. We need to be ready to state the gospel with clarity and boldness.

## GOSPEL OUTLINES
Presenting the gospel in a clear, concise, and compelling way is not as easy as it may sound. It certainly does not just flow

without some forethought. That's why it's worth regularly pausing to think about what we would actually say in a given situation. Whether we've shared the gospel countless times or tend to shy away from it (and most of us are a mixture of the two), it's well worth having a particular concise outline to fall back on. As people called to "always be prepared" (1 Peter 3 v 15), we should be able to state what we believe at a moment's notice. Here's one I often use:

1. *God* is holy and loving,
2. *people* are made in God's image but sinful,
3. *Jesus* died and rose again,
4. and everyone needs to *respond* with repentance and faith.

I used to find reading booklets to people helpful, and would always have some with me, but I no longer find that viable. Most people I know or meet find it odd for me to read a booklet to them. Interestingly, if I show them the exact same content on my phone, scrolling through screen after screen of an app, that doesn't feel odd at all. If that seems more like you, download an app or two for gospel presentation by phone.[86]

I find it best of all, though, to just say what I believe without props. Conversation, I firmly believe, is the best vehicle for evangelism. We all need to develop keen listening and refined conversational skills. We should hone our ability to converse about the weather or how we spend our free time or what books we like to read or why certain movies are our favorites or a dozen other topics as fodder for chit-chat about "lite" topics. Those interactions may pave the way for in-depth discussion about the weightiest topic of all—the message of reconciliation.

Some people will want to discuss or have a further explanation of what we mean by one part of the gospel message but not other parts. Some might be confused by every point.

Most will grasp and even accept some of the message but not all at once. Listening carefully to what they say and watching closely their non-verbal communication will help us zero in on what clogs need to be cleared and help us see how we might seek to encourage them to keep thinking about Jesus—whether that is through another conversation with us, or introducing them to a friend, or inviting them to come to a course for seekers and skeptics such as *Christianity Explored*.

Of course, there is always the temptation to be too wordy and seek to communicate too much. After all, if we catalog every presentation of the good news in the four Gospels as well as in the epistles, we will find tremendous diversity and no single, complete presentation in any one place. If I'm going to insist that every gospel presentation must include mention of the kingdom, God's love, his holiness, his role as Creator, our image-bearing nature, our sin, atonement, and every other non-negotiable point, I will find that no one passage in Scripture follows my plan. As Tim Keller argued, "So yes, there must be one gospel, yet there are clearly different forms in which that one gospel can be expressed."[87]

I rest in the reality that God's kingdom is greater than any gospel presentation I can utter. When Jesus was asked about the nature of the kingdom, he first offered several parables to illustrate it but then posed his own question: "What shall we say the kingdom of God is like, or what parable shall we use to describe it?" (Mark 4 v 30). Think about that for a moment. Jesus wasn't stumped or confused. It's not as if he wasn't smart enough to come up with a way to tell us what he meant. It's that the kingdom, the gospel itself, is so rich, so multifaceted, so immense, so beautiful that no single expression captures it in all its power and size.

Further, I rest in the equally wonderful reality that God uses our proclaiming, however incomplete or flawed, for the saving of lost people. Many times! Every day! We need to point people to the Savior in the Scriptures, proclaim what we can in whatever amount of time God gives us, and trust him to do the impossible work of conversion that only he can do.

That sets us free from the pressure to say all we can possibly say in a minute. It doesn't all ride on that one conversation, and it doesn't all rely on us.

## MAKING THE LINK

Of course, we don't just head straight into our gospel presentation without any preamble. Perhaps we'll already have had plenty of pre-evangelistic conversations like the ones we've imagined in the previous chapters. Or perhaps this is the first one. Either way, we need something that makes the link between the conversation we're having and the gospel we want to proclaim.

We might offer a one-sentence starter, with enthusiasm to match, and see how the Holy Spirit uses it. Think of it as a teaser, if that doesn't sound sacrilegious. Here are some nominees:

"I think we can know God personally."
"I find it a great comfort that I can know God intimately."
"I think we can be sure about life after death."
"I've found something that helps me with guilt or regret."

Sometimes a question starts the conversation best:

"Have you ever considered issues of faith?"
"Do you ever think much about spiritual things?"
"If you could know God in a meaningful way, would you want to?"
"Do you ever wonder what happens after we die?"

We should also be prepared to make a transition statement

that moves the spotlight from them to us. If we've done a good job of listening, this will not sound too bold. Some options are:

"Here's what I believe."
"Here's what Christians believe."
"Let me tell you what Christians hold as their core beliefs."
"Please consider this…"

We point people to the wonder of the gospel and ask God to open their blind eyes to see its beauty. You wouldn't be reading this book or desiring to spread the gospel if God hadn't done that in your own life.

## THE GREATEST PREPARATION

When it comes to evangelizing, we must prepare ourselves to proclaim truth, answer questions, illustrate, explain, and call for a response. But there's something that can help far more. Reveling in wonder at the fullness of the gospel can be the greatest impetus to evangelistic energy. Writer and longtime discipleship mentor Jerry Bridges writes in just about every one of his books, "Preach the gospel to yourself."[88]

C.S. Lewis has helped me grow in my appreciation for the forgiveness God grants us through the cross. Listen to how he contrasted the gospel with a false alternative in the essay "On Forgiveness":

> "I find that when I think I am asking God to forgive me I am often in reality (unless I watch myself very carefully) asking Him to do something quite different. I am asking Him not to forgive me but to excuse me. But there is all the difference in the world between forgiving and excusing. Forgiveness says, 'Yes, you have done this thing, but I accept

*your apology; I will never hold it against you and everything between us two will be exactly as it was before.' But excusing says 'I see that you couldn't help it or didn't mean it; you weren't really to blame.' If one was not really to blame then there is nothing to forgive. In that sense forgiveness and excusing are almost opposites ... If you had a perfect excuse, you would not need forgiveness; if the whole of your action needs forgiveness, then there was no excuse for it. [Our sin] is inexcusable but not, thank God, unforgivable."*[89]

Reading words like these can free us for honest confession, a clear conscience, and bold witness.

We must bask in the greatness of our salvation. As Paul prayed for the Ephesians, we need to ask God to enlighten our eyes "in order that [we] may know the hope to which he has called [us], the riches of his glorious inheritance in his holy people, and his incomparably great power for us who believe" (Ephesians 1 v 18-19). Meditating on and savoring the wonder that the God of the universe chose to save rebels like us is the very best preparation for evangelism—transforming us into bold messengers of the greatest news.

# 6. THE VALUE OF IMAGERY

My childhood house had a vestibule. It's a seldom-used word for a seldom-seen structure. Built onto the outside of a house, it serves as a halfway stop between outside and inside. When my brothers and I returned from a camping trip, my mother insisted we take off our smoky, smelly clothes in the vestibule before entering our house.

When C.S. Lewis criticized secular writers, he snuck in an image: these writers did not "see this world as the vestibule of eternity."[90] Allow that to soak in for a second. Imagine what it means. This world leads to another. It's only temporary: a halfway stop, not a place to settle into. Our real destination lies elsewhere. With this simple phrase, Lewis didn't just inform the intellect; he stirred the imagination.

This highlights the biggest difference between Lewis's evangelistic strategy and most others. He peppered his evangelism with images, so as to enchant, not just explain. I'd be willing to bet that if you knew three lines from Lewis before reading this book, at least two of them contain images rather than propositions. When you read Lewis, you don't just say, "That makes sense." You also add, "That sounds wonderful."

This chapter explores the role of imagination in evangelism because I fear that most outreach fails to engage the heart. We state theologically sound points but fail to go beyond the intellect. Lewis can help us correct this imbalance. Please hear me carefully: I do not want to downplay the importance of sound theology. In our day, shallow theology lurks all around. But I do want to push us in the direction of presenting a multifaceted gospel to multifaceted people.

## LEWIS THE ENCHANTER

C.S. Lewis was a poet at heart. One published collection contains over 100 of his poems. But imagery seeped beyond his poems into all his writings, both fiction and nonfiction. When asked how he came to write *The Lion, the Witch and the Wardrobe*, he said that all seven of his Narnia books "began with seeing pictures in my head. At first, they were not a story, just pictures."[91]

Examples of imagery in his nonfiction abound. For example, in *The Problem of Pain* he likened suffering to God's "megaphone to rouse a deaf world."[92] In *The Weight of Glory* he compared our willingness to settle for the pleasures of this life instead of pursuing the goodness of God to "an ignorant child who wants to go on making mud pies in a slum because he cannot imagine what is meant by the offer of a holiday at the sea."[93] He could have just made the statement "We are far too easily pleased," but that would not have elicited emotions the way images of mud pies and seaside holidays do.

Even Lewis's personal letters teemed with imagery. Just a few months before he died, he slipped into a coma but then revived. When writing to his lifelong friend Arthur Greeves about the experience, he packed his report with numerous images, the last one hitting like the punch line of a joke: "Tho' I am by no means unhappy I can't help feeling it was rather a pity I did revive in July. I mean, having been glided so painlessly up to the Gate it seems hard to have it shut in one's face and know that the whole process must some day be gone thro' again, and perhaps far less pleasantly! Poor Lazarus!"[94]

## WEAVING IMAGES INTO OUR STORY

When you speak of your journey to faith, do you use images? To be sure, we must make clarity and understanding our highest priorities. But sprinkling in images to trigger desire should not be ruled out. My wife begins her story with, "I'm sure you've heard about pirates searching for buried treasure. They don't know exactly where it is but they believe it's out there and it's worth finding. That's how I thought about life for a long time. I knew there was something more and it would be worth finding. I just didn't know where to look." I imagine many people share her experience.

What image might you use? To help you select one, here's a list, compiled by Lewis scholar Michael Ward, of ways in which Lewis described what conversion was like:

> "Becoming a Christian (passing from death to life) is like joining in a campaign of sabotage, like falling at someone's feet or putting yourself in someone's hands, like taking on board fuel or food, like laying down your rebel arms and surrendering, saying sorry, laying yourself open, turning full speed astern; it is like killing part of yourself, like learning to walk or to write, like buying God a present with his own money; it is like a drowning man clutching at a rescuer's hand, like a tin soldier or a statue becoming alive, like waking after a long sleep, like getting close to someone or becoming infected, like dressing up or pretending or playing; it is like emerging from the womb or hatching from an egg; it is like a compass needle swinging to north, or a cottage being made into a palace, or a field being plowed and resown, or a horse turning into a Pegasus, or a greenhouse roof becoming bright in the sunlight; it is like coming around from anesthetic, like coming in out of the wind, like going home."[95]

And let's not forget that Lewis described his own conversion using such pictures as "a soldier unbuckling his protective armor, a snowman beginning to melt, a man being arrested or a fox being hounded, or check and then checkmate in a game of chess."[96]

If Lewis did it, so can we. What is the image that, for you, most naturally describes the experience of becoming a Christian? Get ready to use it in your conversations.

## STEALING PAST THE DRAGONS

Lewis tied his rationale for stirring the imagination to his own experience. In "Sometimes Fairy Stories May Say Best What's to Be Said," he shared, "I saw how stories … could steal past a certain inhibition which had paralysed much of my own religion in childhood … Could one not thus steal past those watchful dragons? I thought one could."[97] Thus, he concluded, "Imagination is the organ of meaning," while "reason [is] the organ of truth."[98] He felt we might reach more people with images than arguments. Or, at least, the imagination served as a better beachhead for a future, logical invasion.

Part of Lewis's motivation to write imaginative works flowed from frustration. Years before writing three science fiction books and a full decade before publishing the first of the *Chronicles of Narnia*, he told J.R.R. Tolkien, "Tollers, there is too little of what we really like in stories. I am afraid we shall have to try and write some ourselves."[99] But their efforts had greater goals than mere entertainment. They both knew that the gateway to the whole person was the emotions and that imaginative fiction could do more than just offer enjoyment.

In *The Lion, the Witch and the Wardrobe*, Lewis retells the gospel story of Jesus' death and resurrection in ways that trigger deep feelings. Tragically, many people have heard this story (or think they have) so many times that it fails to move their emotions. Lewis's transposing of the story onto Aslan, the lion, being tied down onto the stone table and killed, moves readers' emotions so powerfully that many people can't help crying as they read. Listening in as Lucy and Susan weep uncontrollably brings the horror of Jesus' death into the pit of our emotions.

Then there's their joy when Aslan rises:

> *"'You're not a—not a—?' asked Susan in a shaky voice. She couldn't bring herself to say the word ghost. Aslan stooped his golden head and licked her forehead. The warmth of his breath and a rich sort of smell that seemed to hang about his hair came all over her.*
>
> *"'Do I look it?' he said.*
>
> *"'Oh, you're real, you're real! Oh, Aslan!' cried Lucy, and both girls flung themselves upon him and covered him with kisses."* [100]

It wasn't only in evangelism that Lewis employed imagery. It was his weapon of choice for helping Christians grow as well. Even mature believers resist God's pruning work of sanctification from time to time. But they may weaken that resistance when seeing themselves in a well-told story. Once you've read it, can you ever forget the painful process that Eustace went through to become "de-dragoned" in *The Voyage of the Dawn Treader*? His greedy dragonish thoughts in his heart caused him to become a dragon. His horror at seeing his reflection in a pool of water horrifies us as well. And his efforts to shed the dragon's skin never worked, as long as he tried to do it himself. Only by allowing Aslan, his deliverer, to remove the dragon-shell—an excruciating process—could he be restored to his human self.

Straightforward didactic teaching about sin—that it harms me and distorts my personhood—informs me.

Knowing I cannot save myself or produce godly character on my own also helps. But the imagery of Eustace's transformations (from a person into a dragon and then back again) makes me far more repulsed by my sin and even more desirous of God's sanctifying work, no matter how painful the process may be.

Or here's another image Lewis used to describe the transformation process. "You thought you were going to be made into a decent little cottage: but He is building a palace. He intends to come and live in it Himself."[101] A very different illustration, but one which makes readers all the more eager to be refined by God.

Some may be suspicious of all this emphasis on images and the imagination—worrying that it is just emotional manipulation. Lewis anticipated that concern and addressed it this way: "Do you think I am trying to weave a spell? Perhaps I am; but remember your fairy tales. Spells are used for breaking enchantments as well as for inducing them. And you and I have need of the strongest spell that can be found to wake us from the evil enchantment of worldliness which has been laid upon us for nearly a hundred years."[102] He first preached that warning in 1941. Think of how worldliness has mushroomed since then. Sensuality, self-indulgence, materialism and dozens of other "isms" saturate and surround us so thoroughly that we need Lewis's "spell" more than ever.

A psychologist recently published an article in *The Wall Street Journal* about how to help children overcome anxiety and depression. "As a therapist," she began, "I'm often asked to explain why depression and anxiety are so common among children and adolescents. One of the most important explanations—and perhaps the most neglected—is declining interest in religion." She goes on to document that decline and its negative effects on children. "Nihilism is fertilizer for anxiety and depression, and being 'realistic' is overrated. The belief in God—in a protective and guiding figure to rely on when times are tough—is one of the best kinds of support for kids in an increasingly pessimistic world." But what if parents don't believe in God? "I am often asked by parents, 'How do I talk to my child about death if I don't believe in God or heaven?' My answer is always the same: 'Lie.' The idea that you simply die and turn to dust may work for some adults, but it doesn't help children." She goes on to prescribe offering children images of heaven—even if you have to lie!—to counter the bad images all around us in our broken world.[103]

We can do better than that! We can offer images of heaven that are true. We can and we must.

We have a far greater authority than C.S. Lewis for valuing the imagination: the Bible itself. But before we turn to the Scriptures, let's pause for another moment of application. Can you think of an image that expresses how God is working in your life now? In other words, after your conversion, how do you see the gospel at work today? Perhaps you would describe it with images like balm, foundation, lifejacket, comfort, a listening ear, an arm around the shoulder, the best counselor ever, or a best friend forever. You could practice this during a small-group gathering of believers; take turns sharing images or illustrations that capture aspects of your faith. You may find that you spark each other's creativity. Then try out one of these images in a conversation with a non-Christian. Are there people you've been trying to witness to for a long time who seem deaf to your words? Perhaps an image might awaken their spiritual eardrums.

## THE BIBLE'S IMAGE SATURATION

The Bible, too, is full of images. First, there's the narrative nature of the Bible. Some estimate that more than half of

God's word comes through stories. Couldn't God have revealed himself more concisely through a series of proclamations? Of course he could. But he didn't. Why? Because stories engage us as whole persons. They drive home messages more deeply by taking longer. In fact, sometimes it's the length of a story that makes it hit in ways a short lesson couldn't. It's only after I read of Israel's turning away from God—over and over and over again, throughout their history—that I start to examine my own propensity to do the same.

Try this the next time you read a narrative portion of the Scriptures. Ask what a particular story does that a summary statement couldn't. In particular, notice when stories seem to take longer than you think they should and ask why the Master Storyteller chose to inspire his book that way. For example, when Nathan rebukes David for his adultery, he first tells a story that riles David's (and our!) anger (2 Samuel 12). The painful drama of a rich man who had "a very large number of sheep and cattle" stealing and killing a poor man's "one little ewe lamb" sparks readers' righteous indignation better than if the text just said, "Nathan confronted David and told him he had sinned."

Second, there is the poetic nature of the Bible. Poems stir the emotions in ways that prose doesn't. They intensify feelings—of all varieties. The prophets delivered many of their messages in poetry because they wanted changed hearts, not just ritual performance. Israel had already had the straightforward law handed to them. And they had turned away from it. The poetic prophets sought to sneak past watchful dragons to turn rebels back.

Before your next reading of one of the poetic books of the Bible (Job, Ecclesiastes, Psalms, Proverbs, Song of Solomon), or any of the vast poetic sections in the prophets, ask why the message of that particular book or section packs a more potent punch through poetry than it would have through a dissertation. Suffering requires endurance more than understanding, and Job's poetry provides that better than a philosophical treatise. Pose the same question about the meaning of life in Ecclesiastes, the wonder of worship in the Psalms, the perplexities of wise living in Proverbs, and the beauty of marital love in the Song of Solomon. We need poetic images for those aspects of life more than notebooks filled with data.

Third, marvel at how Jesus captivated our whole selves through images. Just for starters, recall his seven I AM statements about himself in John's Gospel: I am the bread of life (6 v 35), the light of the world (8 v 12), the gate (10 v 7), the resurrection and the life (11 v 25), the good shepherd (10 v 11), the way, the truth, and the life (14 v 6), and the vine (15 v 1). Go back over that list now and allow each image to spark emotions. What does each one convey? How might they speak to your non-Christian friends and acquaintances?

Or read through the Gospels and look for the other ways in which Jesus used imagery to teach profound truths. He called his disciples "the salt of the earth" (Matthew 5 v 13) but labeled his opponents "a brood of vipers" (Matthew 12 v 34). He likened his love for Jerusalem to a hen who "gathers her chicks under her wings" (Luke 13 v 34) and God's judgment at the end of time to the moment when a shepherd "separates the sheep from the goats" (Matthew 25 v 32). He spoke of foxes without holes to live in, new wine in old wineskins, a father giving his son a stone instead of bread, specks and planks in eyes—and on and on we could go.

Think of how much less potent Jesus' teaching would have been without his parables. For example, he could have merely told the self-righteous Pharisees that their sin was just as bad as that of the tax collectors and prostitutes. Instead, he told the three parables of the lost sheep, lost coin, and two sons (Luke 15). He contrasted the two brothers drastically. But then he snuck in the rebuke that the older brother disrespected his father just as much as (or more than!) the younger brother. Delaying the punch line of the elder brother's pity party hit far more forcefully than just saying, *Your sins are really bad. Got it?*

Finally, reflect on the variety of images used to describe the gospel in the rest of the New Testament. It is referred to as justification, salvation, regeneration, redemption, propitiation, eternal life, rebirth, reconciliation, and more.[104] If those seem like boring academic terms, unpack what they mean. God pronounces us innocent. He rescues us from disaster. He makes us brand new creatures. He pays for our sins. He gives us a new lease on life—one that never ends. He welcomes us home from all our rebellious wanderings with open arms.

These images do more than just teach a doctrine. And their diversity holds important significance for evangelism. Different people latch on to the gospel at different starting points for different reasons. Some people feel guilty for things they've done. The gospel's message of forgiveness brings freedom to them. Other people feel ashamed of who they are. The gospel's message of adoption grants them a new identity. Some people believe in some kind of God but feel alienated from him. The gospel's offer of reconciliation unites them to the God they've longed for.

Of course, we must also acknowledge and revel in the Bible's straightforward, didactic teaching. The Scriptures come to us in a variety of literary genres. We have the Psalms, Ecclesiastes, and the Song of Solomon, but we also have Romans, Ephesians, and Jude. Jesus told parables, but he also taught theology. So let's not pit imagery against reason or poetry against epistles. All have strengths. All have limits. God inspired them all. And note that all are conveyed through words.

Many people insist that images are better than language. "A picture's worth a thousand words," they love to quip (failing to acknowledge the need for words to make their point). Biblical scholar Peter Adam loved to respond to that cliché with this: "How many pictures would you need to convey that idea?"[105]

## IMAGINATIVE EVANGELISM

If you had to choose one image to share evangelistically, which one might it be? Finding buried treasure? Or getting a clean slate? Or gaining a new status? Or receiving a new name? Or putting on a fresh set of clothes? Or obtaining citizenship of a new country? Try writing this out in just a few sentences. Writing will jump-start and clarify your thinking. Then, try this out in conversations with non-Christians and see if it doesn't pry open a closed heart.

This discussion about imagery also raises the need for waves of new art that exalt the good, the true, and the beautiful. If you sense God's call to explore art, music, film, or other aesthetic careers, press on. Our world desperately needs more Narnias and Middle-earths, more songs, movies, television series, and books that stimulate affections toward heaven rather than tempt flesh toward that other place.

Lewis urged would-be academics to "learn in wartime" (that is, persevere in scholarship) because "to be ignorant and simple now—not to be able to meet the enemies on their own ground—would be to throw down our weapons, and to betray our uneducated brethren who have, under God, no defense but us against the intellectual attacks of the heathen. Good philosophy must exist, if for no other reason, because bad philosophy needs to be answered."[106]

Likewise, good imagery needs to exist, if for no other reason, because bad imagery needs to be countered. Both on a grand scale (producing movies, publishing books, etc.) and on a personal level (weaving imagery into gospel conversations), we need to marshal the creativity God gave us and connect to the longings he's built into us. People just might respond wholeheartedly when they hear the most beautiful story they could have ever imagined.

# 7. THE REALITY OF OPPOSITION

If you look at a short bio on the back of one of C.S. Lewis's books, you'll see that he taught at both Oxford and Cambridge. He spent much more time at Oxford (29 years) and moved to Cambridge only for the last seven years of his career. You may wonder why he made the switch. If you read a fuller biography, you learn that it involved a fair amount of personal pain and no small amount of persecution for his faith.

His Oxford colleagues were not thrilled that he spent so much time speaking in public about religion, which was not his academic specialty. They would have preferred him to publish more academic works, like his magisterial *English Literature in the Sixteenth Century (Excluding Drama),* instead of popular works like *The Problem of Pain* or *The Screwtape Letters.* They certainly frowned upon his writing of children's books.

But Lewis was not naïve about opposition. Fellow Oxford professor J.R.R. Tolkien explained, "Lewis knew this [the persecution he would face] when he accepted the invitation from the BBC and he said … he was driven to do it by his conscience."[107]

Numerous accounts tell how Lewis was shunned by his peers (even some Christians) and passed over many times for promotion at Oxford.[108] Given his many years there, not receiving advancement was a slap in the face. By contrast, Cambridge saw a first-rate scholar worthy of respect and offered him the newly founded Chair in Mediaeval and Renaissance Literature. This prestigious position came with a salary three times what Oxford had been paying him. Even so, Lewis's fond affection for Oxford drove him to decline Cambridge's offer twice before Tolkien finally persuaded him to finish his career at the new location.[109]

## DON'T BE SURPRISED

Like Lewis, we should expect persecution for taking a stand for the gospel. If you're going to pursue mere evangelism, you must prepare for "mere opposition." The Scriptures give us ample warning of hatred and persecution. But still we are surprised by it. Perhaps this is because many of us live in parts of the world where Christianity has been respected or, at least, tolerated for a very long time. But all that is changing right before our eyes as our world moves further and further away from righteousness, moral goodness, and adherence to truth.

Note how people responded to Jesus. When he cast demons out of a man into a herd of pigs, people "pleaded with him to leave their region" (Matthew 8 v 28-34). Apparently, they valued their financial livelihood, provided by the pigs, over the sanity of a human being. When Jesus healed a man on the Sabbath, "the Pharisees went out and began to plot with the Herodians how they might kill Jesus" (Mark 3 v 6). The Pharisees and the Herodians hated each other. Pharisees saw Herodians as oppressors and worthy of scorn. But they preferred to team up with their archenemies to kill Jesus rather than allow him to heal sufferers.

This hatred extended to Jesus' followers—and continues to this very day. The book of Acts is filled with reports of persecutions of the early church. Paul wrote several of his epistles from prison and spoke of being flogged, whipped, beaten with rods, and pelted with stones (2 Corinthians 11 v 23-25). Eventually, he was beheaded for proclaiming the gospel. Other writers of the New Testament urge us to anticipate persecution (e.g. Hebrews 10 v 33) and "not be surprised" by it (1 John 3 v 13 and 1 Peter 4 v 12).

Somehow, we've omitted preparation for persecution from our discipleship efforts. We've failed to prepare new and young Christians for the unfriendly welcome they're likely to receive. To be sure, training in evangelism must center on the standard components—concise statements of the gospel, answers to common questions, ways to clarify our message, calling for a response, etc.

But we must also talk about how to handle rejection.

## FIGHTING BACK

A powerful antidote to opposition from the world flows out of our acceptance in Christ. The love of our Savior strengthens us to handle rejection from outsiders. That's why, when Peter wrote his first letter to encourage a church going through persecution, he began by reminding them of their "living hope through the resurrection of Jesus Christ from the dead, and … an inheritance that can never perish, spoil or fade" (1 Peter 1 v 3-4). They needed to keep this truth in the forefront of their minds, even if "now for a little while you may have had to suffer grief in all kinds of trials" (1 Peter 1 v 6).

In your mind, can you surround expressions of rejection with the wonder of the gospel? Do you see one reality overshadowing the other?[110]

Here's an illustration—that favorite device of C.S. Lewis—which might help. Imagine your total net worth was a mere $100 (pounds or euros or any currency can work) and someone robbed you of $100. That would be devastating. But suppose your net worth was $1 billion and someone robbed you of $100. The actual amount of the loss is the same but the impact differs dramatically. Our net spiritual worth, our riches in Christ, measures in the billions! When someone insults us because of our gospel witness, the hurt might amount to pocket change. If we realize how spiritually rich we are, the loss of someone's positive regard for us can seem as miniscule as a $100 loss to a billionaire.

To be sure, it takes more than just remembering an illustration to gird ourselves up for persecution. Simply telling ourselves, "I can evangelize without fear because I fear God more than I fear people," might not do the trick right away. Certainly, that truth forms the foundation of fearless witness. But we need to allow that concrete to set and harden deep in our souls. That involves rich study of the Scriptures, worship, and meditating on our "fullness" in Christ (see Colossians 2 v 10). We need to "grow in ... grace" (2 Peter 3 v 18).

## A UNIQUE KIND OF OPPOSITION

We cannot ignore a specific form of opposition we encounter today that C.S. Lewis may not have faced: hatred due to our stance against homosexual behavior. Our world has flipped completely from almost universal shunning of homosexuality to explicit praise of it (along with other variations of sexual sin). And anyone who fails to toe the line faces harsh rejection.[111] Antagonism because of our beliefs about God will flow to varying degrees. But condemnation for our beliefs about sex will flood like a tsunami. Because God designed sex to transform people powerfully ("they become one flesh", Genesis 2 v 24), sexual sin distorts people powerfully ("Whoever sins sexually, sins against their own body", 1 Corinthians 6 v 18).

We might try the tactic of stating the objection before our antagonists do. It could sound like this: "I realize the Christian view about sexuality sounds ridiculous in our day and age. I'm fully aware that what the Bible teaches about sex is astonishingly narrow. But God invented sex, and he probably knows how it works best." Lewis modeled this for us in *Mere Christianity*: "Chastity is the most unpopular of the Christian virtues. There is no getting away from it."[112]

Let's not be naïve and assume that such clear thinking on our part will always be received well. Christians have always faced persecution for their stance on biblical morality, whether that was opposition to adultery or denouncing of abortion in the 1st and 2nd centuries, or condemnation of homosexuality today.[113] John the Baptist got his head chopped off after publicly rebuking Herod for "having" his brother's wife (Mark 6 v 18). Christians have always been on the wrong side of history and will continue to be beheaded—figuratively or literally—when they declare God's prescriptions for what people do in bed. However, increasingly, some people who have followed their sexual desires in biblically forbidden ways have realized that the results were not as fulfilling as promised.[114] We can trust that some disappointed people may someday, by the grace of God, embrace teaching they once scoffed at.

At some point, wisdom should lead us to divert the conversation from homosexuality back toward the gospel. It could sound like this: "The Bible teaches that we all have a much deeper problem than any sexual practice. It's our rebellion against God. That messes everyone up in all sorts of ways, including our sexuality." Or, we could offer, "Actually, everyone—gay or straight—has had their sexuality distorted by sin. That's a bigger issue than who we sleep with."

## WHEN WE OBSTRUCT OURSELVES

But the world is not the only source of obstacles to outreach. The Bible warns us to expect opposition from three sources: the world, the flesh, and the devil. Each poses unique challenges for evangelism. We've already explored the world's persecution. Let's now turn to our own fleshly nature—which can attack our gospel proclamation not only by making us afraid but also by leading us into pride and insecurity.

Pride can look like this. If we get into spiritual conversations with non-Christians, we may become impatient with them. "How can they not understand this? It's so obvious!" We don't say it out loud (hopefully!), but underneath, we begin to wonder, "Why can't they have the same good sense that I have and accept Jesus as their Lord and Savior?" I hope you sense the irony of taking pride in having accepted forgiveness for sin!

C.S. Lewis once confessed that he did not like to preach (evangelistically or otherwise) too often because, after each time, "I had to get to my knees pretty quickly, to kill the deadly sin of pride."[115] There's something about the proclaiming of truth that sets us up for taking credit for that truth. Pride takes many forms. They're all bad.

One helpful way to deal with pride is to laugh at it. Lewis helps us tremendously with his comic treatment of pride in *The Screwtape Letters*. Remember, this is a correspondence from a senior demon to a young demonic trainee:

> *"Your patient has become humble; have you drawn his attention to this fact? All virtues are less formidable to us once the man is aware that he has them, but this is specially true of humility. Catch him at the moment when he is really poor in spirit and smuggle into his mind the gratifying reflection, 'By jove! I'm being humble,' and almost immediately pride— pride at his own humility—will appear. If he awakes to the danger and tries to smother this new form of pride, make him proud of his attempt—and so on, through as many stages as you please. But don't try this too long, for fear you awake his sense of humour and proportion, in which case he will merely laugh at you and go to bed."*[116]

At the other end of the fleshly spectrum from pride we find insecurity. You may think this is just another word for fear. But, as I'm using the terms here, fear is sparked from the outside ("What will people think of me?") while insecurity wells up from within ("I don't have what it takes to proclaim good news"). You might feel insecure because you don't know enough answers to questions people might pose. Or you might feel inadequate because you're not a smooth communicator. Or you might feel a lack of confidence due to your own moral failures. For most Christians, the very task of evangelism tends to breed insecurity.

C.S. Lewis experienced these struggles as well. His context was public debate, but his comments apply to anyone who engages in gospel conversations with non-believers: "I have found that nothing is more dangerous to one's own faith than the work of an apologist. No doctrine of that Faith seems to me so spectral, so unreal as one that I have just successfully defended in a public debate. For a moment, you see, it has seemed to rest on oneself: as a result, when you go away from that debate, it seems no stronger than that weak pillar."[117]

Release from insecurity comes when we turn our focus away from ourselves to the message we proclaim. To be sure, we need to prepare for answering questions. But we must never trust in our ability to answer those questions. We must think through the best way to word things, but we can never place our confidence in those words, no matter how eloquently we string them together. Our confidence is not in our confidence.

When I present seminars on evangelism, someone inevitably asks, "What happens if someone asks me a question I don't know how to answer?" I always respond, "Count on it! It's guaranteed! It's not a matter of "if" someone will ask a question you can't answer; it's "when." We must trust ultimately in the truthfulness and power of our message, no matter how poorly we might stammer through it. Acknowledging that we don't know an answer won't harm our outreach as much as we fear. In fact, it bolsters our efforts by causing us to model humility—which is what our inquirers need in order to receive the free gift of salvation. And it gives us an opportunity to go away, research the answer, and come back to start a new conversation about Jesus.

Perhaps your flesh resists evangelizing for other reasons than fear, pride, or insecurity. Is it anger? Lack of compassion? Guilt? Whatever form it takes, don't neglect prayerful investigation into what lurks within. Then, diligently apply the gospel's double power of forgiveness and cleansing (1 John 1 v 9) to that particular sin. Then, you'll shine as both a proclaimer and a displayer of the gospel's transforming power.

## VICTORY IN THE BATTLE

Our three antagonists—the world, the flesh, and the devil—do work together rather well. At times, it's hard to determine where the pushback comes from. The need to stand strong applies in many directions for numerous attacks. Lewis portrayed the interplay of the flesh and the devil most powerfully in *The Screwtape Letters*. He commented, "Some have paid me an undeserved compliment by supposing that my Letters were the ripe fruit of many years' study in moral and ascetic theology. They forgot that there is an equally reliable, though less creditable, way of learning how temptation works. 'My heart'—I need no other's—'showeth me the wickedness of the ungodly.'"[118]

In one sense, then, it doesn't matter whether it's the world trying to conform us to its pattern (Romans 12 v 2), or our flesh worshiping something other than God (Ephesians 5 v 5), or the devil prowling around like a roaring lion looking to devour us (1 Peter 5 v 8). We just need to prepare for a struggle.

One aid for the spiritual battle is to remember the different names in the Bible for the devil. He's called our "enemy"

(1 Peter 5 v 8), meaning he hates us and wants to harm us. He's called "the father of lies" (John 8 v 44) and contradicts God's truth in seemingly limitless ways. He's referred to as an "angel of light" (2 Corinthians 11 v 14), making evil things look appealing and harmless. He's called "the god of this age" (2 Corinthians 4 v 4) and uses incessant distractions, sensual temptations, and promises of power to blind us from seeing the truth. And in one verse, he's identified as both "the ruler of the kingdom of the air" and "the spirit who is now at work in those who are disobedient" (Ephesians 2 v 2). Note the disastrous cooperation of forces from without and within in just those two phrases.

It's worth pausing to ask yourself: Under which alias does the devil attack me most frequently? Where am I most susceptible to his schemes? What truth do I need to meditate on to counter his lies?

The greatest aid for victory in spiritual battle comes from donning the armor of God (Ephesians 6 v 10-17). It's easy to simply move past this passage if we know it well, but it pays to take extensive time to study, memorize, meditate on, and discuss these rich verses—applying them to all aspects of our lives, especially in relevance to the task of evangelism. Just to prime the pump, reflect on these brief insights about the individual pieces of armor.

The belt buckled around your waist—the very center of your body—is truth. How might you make truth central to your life? What lies bombard you regularly? From where do they come? How can you make reading and meditating on the Scriptures non-negotiable, ever-increasing parts of your daily routine?

The breastplate—which protects your heart—is righteousness. Are you fluent in reminding yourself of your right standing before God because of the finished work of the cross? Can you identify other "identities" that compete with your status as a child of God? Do you see how false identities harm your heart rather than protect it?

The parts that fit on your feet—helping you move forward—involve "readiness that comes from the gospel of peace." Does the good news so enamor you that it sends you? Have you so relished the fact that we have peace with God that you want to tell others how good that is? Can you articulate the gospel message by quoting a few key verses and offering a few illustrations?

The shield—which extinguishes flaming arrows from the evil one—is faith. Do you really believe and rely on the proclamation that "greater is He who is in you than he who is in the world" (1 John 4 v 4 NASB) and that if you "resist the devil … he will flee from you" (James 4 v 7)?

The helmet—which protects your head, the command center of your thinking—is salvation. God poured out his wrath on his Son instead of on you, so you can be saved, spared from disaster, delivered out of darkness, and rescued from spending eternity separated from all the goodness of God. Does that marvelous truth dominate your thoughts?

The sword of the Spirit—the only offensive weapon in the set—is the word of God. Does biblical truth and thinking Christianly shape your perspective more than any other philosophy, worldview, or idea? Do you study the Scriptures with others in your church so that "iron sharpens iron" (Proverbs 27 v 17)? When you see lies, do you know what God's word says instead?

So much more could be said. Indeed, much more needs to be deeply ingrained in us so we remember that "our struggle is not against flesh and blood [other people], but against the rulers, against the authorities, against the powers of this dark world and against the spiritual forces of evil in the heavenly realms" (Ephesians 6 v 12).

When you start reading *The Screwtape Letters*, you think,

"This will be fun! I'm in for a lot of laughs!" Then, just a few pages in, you realize this is no joke. In a similar way, you may have imagined evangelism to be a fun adventure. Then you find out it's not as easy as you thought. But people's lives are too sacred to opt out when the going gets tough. Your efforts—no matter how hard fought—could make a difference forever.

Screwtape knew how high the stakes are. Let us soberly remember his dark insight: "In the long run either Our Father [the devil] or the Enemy [God] will say 'mine' of each thing that exists, and specially of each man. They will find out in the end, never fear, to whom their time, their souls, and their bodies really belong—certainly not to them, whatever happens. At present the Enemy says 'mine' of everything on the pedantic, legalistic ground that He made it. Our Father hopes in the end to say 'mine' of all things on the more realistic and dynamic ground of conquest."[119]

# 8. THE POWER OF PRAYER

Lyle Dorsett is one of the most knowledgeable experts today about Lewis's life and works. He served as the director of Wheaton College's Marion E. Wade Center, a repository of writings of Lewis and six other influential writers, for seven years. He gathered hundreds of hours of oral histories of friends of C. S. Lewis and has written several volumes about him and his wife, Joy Davidman. His career includes over 20 years of teaching about Lewis and evangelism at Wheaton College and Beeson Divinity School of Samford University. Many also know him for his shepherding gifts through personal discipleship at the schools where he taught and the churches where he pastored. I'm grateful for the friendship God has forged between Lyle and myself over the past few years.

What people may not know is that Dorsett used to be an angry, alcoholic agnostic who, by his own admission, was "aggressively anti-Christian" and "loved to make fun of Christians, putting them down as bigots." He rose to academic success quickly, completing a Ph.D. in history in less than three years and landing a teaching position before the age of 30. But, like so many, success did not satisfy him. Even a happy marriage and the gifts of two young children couldn't keep him away from alcohol—large quantities of it. He told me he got drunk most weekends and several nights during the week.

So when his wife, who had recently become a Christian, asked him not to drink in their house for fear of setting a bad example for the children, Dorsett stormed out, got in his car and drove to where people wouldn't condemn him for drinking—a bar. He drank until closing time, then took a six-pack of beer to go. The bartender told him to drive home carefully.

Hearing Dorsett tell the story caused me to marvel at the protective power of God. Lyle drove down "a curvaceous mountain road" that had claimed the lives of many sober people over the years. What he remembers is not remembering. "I have absolutely no recollection of what happened between the time I left that bar and when woke up several hours later in my car, parked in a cemetery." The sight of tombstones must have sobered him up in a hurry. "I should have been killed. How did I get off that road alive?" he thought. Then, "I may not be dead but I'm dying."

He prayed, "God, if you're there, will you help me?" As he drove home, he wondered what his wife would think about his being out all night—if she'd even be there at all. But he also had a sense of peace—an experience he describes as "having Jesus sitting right next to me in the passenger seat of that car. And I knew he loved me!"

He was not unfamiliar with the gospel message. The sowing process had begun over ten years before, when an undergraduate student challenged his agnostic ideas.

"Professor Dorsett," he asked one day, "Did you say that no intelligent person would ever be a Christian?" Dorsett clarified, "I said, no *thoughtful* intelligent person would ever be a Christian" (as if the distinction made a difference). "Have you ever read anything by G.K. Chesterton or C.S. Lewis?" the student challenged him. Dorsett admitted he had not. The next day the student presented his professor with a brand new copy of Chesterton's *Orthodoxy*. "He didn't have the kind of money to buy that," Dorsett told me, more than 40 years later. The student signed it and doodled a picture under his signature—an odd image of a tomb with a stone rolled away from its opening. The student explained its Christian significance and added, "I always draw that picture under my signature." He wrote in the book, "To Dr. Dorsett, with the prayer that this book would move you toward orthodoxy."

Lyle had read the book but not found it convincing—yet. Now, though, as he arrived home after his drunken drive down the mountain, some of what he read there came to the forefront of his thinking.

"When I got home, I told my wife, 'Something has happened to me.'" She simply replied, "I can tell." That Sunday, he went to church with his family. But this time it seemed dramatically different than his previous attendances. After hearing his story, the pastor said, "Sir, you owe it to yourself to read *Mere Christianity*." Lyle did. And he now says that it was the tool God used to solidify his newfound saving faith.

A decade later, while serving as the director of The Wade Center, he received a letter from someone inquiring about the writings of George MacDonald. It came from a man who was on furlough from his work as a missionary in China. Under his signature, he had doodled a picture of a tomb with a stone rolled away from its opening! Yes, it was indeed that very same former student who had given Lyle the copy of *Orthodoxy* many years before. As you might imagine, their reconnection brought tears to both men's eyes. Lyle choked up telling me about it. He added, "I've been a firm believer in the efficacy of prayer ever since."

Make no mistake: prayer takes devotion, steadfastness, and "stick-to-it-iveness." C.S. Lewis's example can help us. The Bible can help even more. Let's look at both, starting with the Oxford professor.

## A DIFFICULT PRACTICE

As I read Lewis, certain themes bubble up to the top. I see them in his fiction and nonfiction, in his books and essays, in his letters and in recollections by friends. One major, recurring theme is the topic of prayer. Many of his letters mention his prayers for the recipients as well as including requests for prayers for himself. He did not shy away from the topic in one of his earliest books, *The Problem of Pain*, nor in *Mere Christianity*, even though both were evangelistic works, where other writers would have avoided such a thorny issue.[120] He also addressed the topic repeatedly in *The Screwtape Letters*, where the demon Screwtape calls it "the painful subject of prayer."[121]

Perhaps Lewis's repeated return to the topic flowed from his own struggles with prayer. He admitted that his long-held atheism emerged from the horror of unanswered prayer for healing for his dying mother. Fifty years later, when a Christian, he wrote of how God answered a prayer for healing for "a woman whose thighbone was eaten through with cancer and who had thriving colonies of the disease in many other bones as well."[122] We assume he's referring to his wife, Joy. But later her cancer returned. When Lewis put into words the aches of mourning her loss, he observed, "Go to Him when your need is desperate, when all other help is vain, and what do you find? A door slammed in your face, and a sound of bolting and double bolting on the inside. After that silence."[123] It's helpful to read about prayer from someone who admits the difficulties so honestly. The more I read about Lewis's prayer life, the more I want to press on. If he could persevere in prayer, even experiencing all the suffering and pain he did, I can do the same.

What of his prayers for the unconverted? In one place Lewis reports, "I have two lists of names in my prayers, those for whose conversion I pray, and those for whose conversion

I give thanks. The little trickle of transferences from List A to List B is a great comfort."[124] Sheldon Vanauken, a writer who had many interchanges about the gospel with Lewis, reported how his mentor responded when he finally became a Christian: "My prayers are answered."[125]

The key point here is that prayer takes perseverance—and that is especially true when it comes to praying for the salvation of lost souls. If ever there are temptations to quit and question prayer's efficacy, it's when we plead with God to return prodigals and what we hear in response sounds like a door slammed in our face.

Lewis's devotion to prayer was fueled by the same level of intellectual reflection as his apologetics. He applied rigorous rumination to the questions of why and how we should pray. His *Letters to Malcolm: Chiefly on Prayer* contains a gold mine of wisdom on the topic. Lewis had tried to write a straightforward, didactic book on prayer at least one other time and found it too difficult.[126] But when he adopted the mode of a fictitious series of letters (just as he had done in *The Screwtape Letters*), the project succeeded. He also offers deep theological and practical lessons in *Reflections on the Psalms*, especially about the crucial component of praise.

At the same time, Lewis humbly admitted the limits of our intellect in unraveling certain puzzles about prayer. He quoted the 17th-century thinker Blaise Pascal: "'God,' said Pascal, 'instituted prayer in order to lend to His creatures the dignity of causality.'"[127] It is good to know that our prayers can make a difference. Yet Lewis also admitted that prayer's efficacy is not something that can be proved: "a compulsive empirical proof such as we have in the sciences can never be attained."[128]

By affirming both prayer's power and its mystery, Lewis provided the encouragement we need to remain steadfast in prayer, even if we can't explain all the ways it works. He liked the word "efficacy" when talking about prayer, yet resisted the temptation to reduce it to a formula or mechanics. We are not saying magic words that have a guaranteed outcome, nor are we "using" God to gain our own selfish wishes.

Lewis did not shy away from addressing the thorny issue of unanswered prayer. Some think the only reason why prayers go unanswered is due to a lack of faith on the part of the petitioner. Here is Lewis's most potent rebuttal to that idea: "In Gethsemane the holiest of all petitioners prayed three times that a certain cup might pass from Him. It did not. After that the idea that prayer is recommended to us as a sort of infallible gimmick may be dismissed."[129] If Jesus did not get his prayer in Gethsemane answered, it surely was not because of a lack of faith.

Lewis elsewhere turns the question of unanswered prayer on its head. "In our ignorance we ask what is not good for us or for others, or not even intrinsically possible. Or again, to grant one man's prayer involves refusing another's. There is much here which it is hard for our will to accept but nothing that is hard for our intellect to understand."[130]

Putting it more positively and perhaps more helpfully, Tim Keller echoes Lewis with this: "In short, God will either give us what we ask or give us what we would have asked if we knew everything he knew."[131]

Even with Keller's optimistic insight, prayer is difficult or, as Lewis put it, "irksome." With his usual honesty, he confessed, "An excuse to omit [prayer] is never unwelcome. When it is over, this casts a feeling of relief and holiday over the rest of the day. We are reluctant to begin. We are delighted to finish. While we are at prayer, but not while we are reading a novel or solving a cross-word puzzle, any trifle is enough to distract us."[132]

And yet he did not quit. Nor should we. In a way that acknowledges all the difficulties, frustrations, conundrums, and pain, Lewis propels us to diligence in prayer: "The painful effort which prayer involves is no proof that we are doing something we were not created to do. If we were perfected, prayer would not be a duty, it would be delight. Some day, please God, it will be."[133]

Lewis helps us in our prayer lives because he's a fellow struggler. Some books on prayer discourage, leaving us to think, "Well, I'm glad that guy has such a vibrant, consistent, effective, struggle-free, answer-filled prayer life. I doubt I will ever experience anything close to that." By contrast, Lewis thought of himself as a fellow pupil in the school of prayer. In the introduction to his *Reflections on the Psalms*, he explained amusingly, "When you took the problem to a master, as we all remember, he was very likely to explain what you understood already, to add a great deal of information which you didn't want, and say nothing at all about the thing that was puzzling you ... the fellow-student can help more than the master because he knows less."[134]

We benefit from looking to Lewis for encouragement in prayer in at least three ways: We observe and appreciate his practice of prayer (diligent and lifelong). We reflect on his thoughtfulness about prayer (deep yet humble). We acknowledge and accept his honesty about prayer (it's difficult but worth it). Let's take these lessons with us as we look to an even better source for a fruitful prayer life—the Bible.

## PERILS AND POTENTIAL

This is certainly not the place to explore all the complexities of the Bible's teachings about prayer. It is definitely not the place to try to unravel the mysterious connections between God's sovereignty and people's intercessions.[135] But I do hope to shine a spotlight on some of the Bible's encouragements for us to persevere in prayer for people's salvation.

Following Lewis's example, we might begin by thinking deeply about prayer. At first, prayer seems easy. What could be more natural than conversing with our God? Once we experience salvation, there is no longer a great gulf separating us from God. He hears our prayers and, because of the shed blood of our Savior, we can "approach God's throne of grace with confidence" (Hebrews 4 v 16). Prayer is simply conversing with God, who in Christ is already always interceding for us and will never leave us. We're given 150 Psalms as examples and templates for our prayers, as well as many other recorded prayers that model how we can express the most crucial words we can ever utter.

But when we get past our initial study and move into practice, we begin to understand Lewis's choice of the word "irksome." We struggle with this seemingly easy discipline. At times we grope to find the words or, worse, the motivation. Perhaps part of our problem comes from unrealistic expectations about prayer. We assume it will be easy and, when it's not, we wonder what's wrong with us.

But if we, like Lewis, persevere in the practice of prayer and in our thoughtfulness about prayer, we find that the Bible itself acknowledges the difficulties. Paul urged the Colossians to "devote" themselves to prayer and offered two helps to make it slightly less difficult: "being watchful and thankful" (Colossians 4 v 2). Why use the word "devote" if the process is easy? Why the need to watch (paying attention to how God begins to answer) if that would be obvious? Why the admonition to be thankful (making note of how and when God answers) if we had no tendency to forget? Later in the same letter, Paul said that his fellow-believer Epaphras was "always wrestling in prayer" for the Colossian Christians (4 v 12). Wrestling doesn't sound like a metaphor for something easy.

When Jesus taught about prayer in his Sermon on the Mount, he began by cautioning against wrong ways to go about it before offering specific words to use. Apparently, it's easy to fall into sub-biblical traps. We could pray to impress others, as Pharisees do (Matthew 6 v 1, 5), or to manipulate God, as pagans do (v 7). In contrast to both these approaches, Jesus gave us the Lord's Prayer—the greatest prayer of all, intended both as words to repeat (Luke 11 v 2: "When you pray, say…") and as a template for our own wording (Matthew 6 v 9: "This, then, is how you should pray…").

When requested, "Lord, teach us to pray," Jesus did not dismiss the question with, *Oh, come on. It's easy. All you have to do is talk to God.* Instead—besides giving us the Lord's Prayer—he told a parable that urges us to keep praying, even with "shameless audacity" (Luke 11 v 8). He drove the point home with the images of asking, seeking, and knocking. Jesus told another parable—this one about a persistent widow—with the explicit purpose that we "should always pray and not give up" (Luke 18 v 1).

Jesus wanted us to remember the perils of prayer. But he also wanted us to grasp the potential of prayer. He said our prayers must include "Your kingdom come, your will be done, on earth as it is in heaven" (Matthew 6 v 10). That means there must be a strong cause-effect connection between our prayers and God's kingdom. While it's tempting to settle for a weak view of prayer ("Our prayers don't change anything but they do change us"), Jesus won't endorse that. He wouldn't have told us to pray, "Your kingdom come" if it made no difference.

## PRESSING ON IN PRAYER

If C.S. Lewis was right that prayer can be "irksome" and Jesus warned that we might lose heart, how can we "devote" ourselves to this kingdom-advancing practice? Here are three suggestions, with particular focus on prayer's connection to evangelism. You may well have heard or even put into practice suggestions like these before—but let me encourage you to consider your approach afresh as you read.

First, we need a system. Spontaneous prayer is nice and certainly an important part of Christian living ("pray continually," 1 Thessalonians 5 v 17). But remaining steadfast in prayer won't happen casually. We need a set time (or times) each day and, ideally, a set place. For many, it's early in the morning. For others, that's the worst time. Figure out what has the best potential to work for you. But then anticipate a million excuses or distractions or interruptions that will threaten that sacred part of your schedule. You'll have to fight to keep it an immovable priority.

Once we have that prayer schedule set, we need to devise a system where non-Christians' names appear regularly. Some people have a section in their prayer journal with a list of names. Some use index cards. Some look at photos. The point is, if we're going to pray for our needs ("daily bread"), forgiveness of sins ("our debts"), and wisdom for the day, we must also include pleading for lost prodigals to come to their senses (see Luke 15 v 17).

We need to pray for both groups and individuals. Paul told us he prayed for "Israelites" (Romans 10 v 1), but he also modeled prayer for individuals when he said he was praying for King Agrippa and all those listening to him (Acts 26 v 29). Newsletters from missionaries or a guide for prayers for the entire world, such as *Operation World*, help get our attention off ourselves and onto a very large world that needs a very great Savior.[136] Asking God to lift our eyes to the harvest all around us can energize our prayers and prompt evangelistic efforts.

It's easy to forget that "salvation comes from the Lord" (Jonah 2 v 9). We regress from prayer ("Holy Spirit, please convict my friend of her need for you") to scheming ("I'll give her that book, share that diagram, send her that link to that website"). We must take action. But prayer comes first, including asking God for wisdom for the next steps to take and the best words to say (James 1 v 5).

Second, we must start with fixing our attention on the one to whom we're praying. Have you noticed that, in the Lord's Prayer, the entire first half is all about God? Only after reminding ourselves that he is our Father in heaven, whose name is holy and whose kingdom is advancing, do we turn our attention to our daily bread and other needs.

Spend time addressing God by name and choose different names than just your favorite default titles. When asking God to draw wandering people back to himself, use a title like "Shepherd of Israel" or "God of Abraham, Isaac, and Jacob." That can bolster our confidence that God is gracious—even toward those who disobey and make a mess of their lives.

Third, we must see distractions as opportunities rather than obstacles. When other people flit in and out of your mind, pray for them. Perhaps it was God himself who brought to mind that guy in your neighborhood or that friend you haven't called in years. Maybe they're not interruptions but additions to your prayer list.

Consider this phenomenon from the point of view of the devil, who wants to stop you from praying—as imagined by Lewis in *The Screwtape Letters*, where one demon gives advice to another on how to lure a Christian away from "the Enemy" (God).

> *"When [a] distraction crosses [the Christian's] mind you ought to encourage him to thrust it away by sheer will power and to try to continue the normal prayer as if nothing had happened; once he accepts the distraction as his present problem and lays that before the Enemy and makes it the main theme of his prayers and his endeavours, then, so far from doing good, you have done harm. Anything, even a sin, which has the total effect of moving him close up to the Enemy makes against us in the long run."* [137]

We need to focus more on the power of prayer and less on its irksomeness. We need to work at prayer rather than know how it works. We need to remain steadfast in it and not lose heart. Perhaps, in God's mercy and grace, he will involve our intercessions with his irresistible grace, and many will be moved toward orthodoxy.

# 9. THE TIMELINESS OF PUSHBACK

Having the same name as someone famous provides great amusement for me. Perhaps you know the musician Randy Newman, who wrote the music to the *Toy Story* movies and its signature hit "You've Got a Friend in Me." People email me, thinking I'm that Randy Newman. They tell me how much they love my music, how happy they were when I won the Academy Award, and how very, very, very much they want me to get *their* songs heard around the world. One guy even invited me to sing "You've Got a Friend in Me" at his daughter's wedding.

I usually reply with something like this: "If you take a closer look at my website, you'll see that I'm a different Randy Newman than the guy who wrote the music to *Toy Story* and other fun songs. I help people with a different story—the one where their life story connects to God's story."

Most people never respond. A few send a brief apology for bothering me. Some share their own religious perspectives, which range from traditional Christianity to some rather creative theories on the meaning of life. A handful of responses have led to some very engaging conversations about the gospel.

For several months, I've been in dialogue with an atheist professor of mathematics who first contacted me to tell me how much he likes my music. Our conversation has been cordial, respectful, and sincere. One day, he sent a rather sarcastic email, totally out of character with his other notes. It was brief, but it stung: "Here's something Christians need to own up to. Why are there so many different kinds of Christianity? There isn't more than one kind of mathematics. There isn't more than one kind of biology. There isn't more than one kind of physics."

I wrestled with how to reply. I opted for my favorite technique—asking questions—with an added touch of some pushback. I wrote, "Are you saying there isn't disagreement within the academic disciplines of mathematics or biology or physics? Do all scholars in these fields agree on all details of their discipline? I'm surprised to see such a simplistic question from someone with Ph.D. level training and experience. Was that a sincere question or a jab at me?"

I wondered if I had pushed back too hard. (My wife says I tend to do that.) I prayed that God would use my words, even if they hurt him in some way. I've erred on both sides of this razor's edge many times. I've struck back when I should have shut up, and I've rolled over and played dead when I should have turned the tables. I have no easy formula for finding the right balance. But Scripture does tell us to beware of "throwing our pearls to pigs" (Matthew 7 v 6). We've got to figure out what that means if we're going to effectively preach the gospel in our skeptical age.

We'll dig into these concepts below. But first, let me tell you how my conversation partner responded. Here's what he wrote:

> *"First, and most important—I may occasionally express myself inartfully, but it is never my intent to jab you. If I have seemed to do so, I sincerely apologize. I am thoroughly enjoying my conversation with you, and if I am clumsy in expression, I am deeply sorry.*

> *"While it is certainly true that scientists squabble at the edges of their fields while the field progresses, they lay behind them something common. Perhaps I am answering my own challenge; that the diversity of Christianity is really no different from the diversity at the edge of scientific progress. Huh. That puts me on my heels. Thanks for challenging me, Randy. I've learned something new today, thanks to you."*

Sometimes the pushback works! But we need greater motivation than mere pragmatism for responding to inquirers. Our words must honor God in every way—in their meaning and tone, their content and intent, their selection and delivery. This takes wisdom in the moment and, more importantly, a soft heart before we start to speak. This chapter serves as the other side of the coin laid out in chapter 3, where we explored honoring objections. Sometimes we honor objections with a gentle rebuke.

C.S. Lewis was a master of pushback. We'll look more closely at some examples below. But to begin with, we should allow ourselves to be brought up short by his willingness to disagree. "But this is not true," he said bluntly about one anti-Christian argument.[138] He was not afraid to differ, to rebuke, or to warn his audiences about the path they were heading down.

## FINDING THE BALANCE

You may resist this notion. It sounds unkind, doesn't it? It can be. But it doesn't have to be. Consider God's two-sided prescription in Proverbs 26 v 4-5. In what seems, at first, like a contradiction, the Scriptures proclaim:

> *Do not answer a fool according to his folly, or you yourself will be just like him.*

*Answer a fool according to his folly, or he will be wise in his own eyes.*

The first proverb guards against falling into the same foolish mire as our antagonist. If he or she uses sarcasm and we respond with sarcasm, then we are just two fools. On the other hand, we are to answer a fool "according to his folly" or "as his folly deserves" (NASB). This must mean we need wise responses, so our attacker doesn't presume they are the wise one. I hope my exchange with my math professor friend embodied the teaching of this proverb.

Have you ever had someone challenge what you've said or believe? Has anyone ever told you you're wrong? What have those experiences been like for you on the receiving end? Hopefully, you've had a friend who cares enough to point you in a different direction when you're heading for some kind of cliff. Ideally, they challenged you kindly. When we feel attacked, we rarely respond well.

Let's apply this in the opposite direction—toward you as the challenger. Do you tend to clam up and say nothing when you could push back? Or are you one who loves an argument and engages in conflict at the drop of a hat? Neither extreme is best. We need to find a balance between "Wounds from a friend can be trusted" (Proverbs 27 v 6) and "A gentle answer turns away wrath" (Proverbs 15 v 1).

One of my friends regularly says these words to me: "I disagree." He listens respectfully and never interrupts. Sometimes he says, "I think you're right." But "I disagree" has become a regular feature in his words to me. He follows them with long pauses, waits to see how I respond, and then elaborates on why I should consider changing my mind. I value his friendship immensely.

## JESUS' SUPREME MODEL OF PUSHBACK

Our Savior exemplifies supreme wisdom in this regard. But his example sometimes shocks us. Have you heard people talk about Jesus as "meek and mild?" This seems at odds with what we read in the Gospels. To be sure, Jesus did say many things about loving our neighbor and turning the other cheek. But consider his barrage of "woes" to those he called "hypocrites" (seven times!), "blind guides," "blind fools," "whitewashed tombs," "snakes," and a "brood of vipers" (Matthew 23).

It wasn't just his opponents that Jesus challenged. When James and John asked for special seating arrangements in heaven, Jesus said, "You don't know what you are asking" (Mark 10 v 38). Even his own mother got a little pushback—at a wedding of all places! When Mary pointed out that they had run out of wine, Jesus' first words were, "Woman, why do you involve me?" (John 2 v 4)

You may be tempted to think, "Well, that's ok for Jesus. He's Jesus! Shouldn't we reserve that kind of behavior for the Messiah?" Remember, however, that he taught us, "Do not give dogs what is sacred; do not throw your pearls to pigs" (Matthew 7 v 6). Jesus wants us to know that some people have closed their hearts to truth. No matter how clearly we explain the gospel or how patiently we offer reasons for belief, they will remain impenetrable. As painful as it seems, we need to know when not to waste our breath by carefully restating our arguments. There must be times when confronting people fits better than straightforward answers. Paul taught that our task includes "demolish[ing] arguments and every pretension that sets itself up against the knowledge of God" (2 Corinthians 10 v 5). Sometimes we need to say, "I think you're wrong. I hope you'll reconsider this."

When I present workshops on evangelism, participants often ask about Jesus' words in Matthew 10 v 14: "If anyone will not welcome you or listen to your words, leave that home or town and shake the dust off your feet." Are there times when we should give up and turn our evangelistic attention elsewhere? My response is to apply that passage to our situations very rarely, if ever. Given all the other instructions Jesus gave to the Twelve in that instance (Matthew 10 v 1-10) and the extremity of the persecution he envisioned (Matthew 10 v 16-31), I'm inclined to think their situation was historically and evangelistically unique. Shaking the dust off one's feet expressed strong condemnation in Jesus' day. We can apply the wisdom of Proverbs, even refusing to answer a fool in his folly, without the need for such extreme measures.

## ARTFUL ARGUMENT FROM THE OXFORD DON

C.S. Lewis modeled disagreement in a variety of very helpful ways. Sometimes, he just declared that some ideas were wrong. Early in *Mere Christianity* he anticipated the objection against universal morality. "I know some people say ... different civilisations and different ages have had quite different moralities." He simply followed (as we saw earlier in this chapter) with "But this is not true." Only after drawing this hard line in the sand did he offer support for his strong claim.

When contrasting Christian faith to a popular alternative, he boldly declared, "You must not think that I am putting forward any heathen fancy of being absorbed into Nature. Nature is mortal; we shall outlive her. When all the suns and nebulae have passed away, each one of you will still be alive."[139]

Sometimes he softened his words when others might have sharpened theirs. This works especially well when countering common misconceptions about the gospel. For example, when Lewis addressed the view that Christianity is just a bunch of rules to follow and tick off, he gently responded, "I do not think that is the best way of looking at it. I would much rather say that every time you make a choice you are turning the central part of you, the part of you that chooses, into something a little different from what it was before."[140]

In some instances, his brilliant reasoning skills allowed him to dismantle arguments before offering the truth. Such was the case when he famously responded to the claim that Jesus was just a good man but not God. "A man who was merely a man and said the sort of things Jesus said would not be a great moral teacher. He would either be a lunatic—on the level with the man who says he is a poached egg—or else he would be the Devil of Hell. You must make your choice."[141] He also took on the idea that Jesus never claimed to be God. Some have claimed it was only his disciples who invented those statements. Lewis responded, "The theory only saddles you with twelve inexplicable lunatics instead of one."[142]

Of course, when responding to less-than-sincere objections, he felt no need to mince words. "There is no need to be worried by facetious people who try to make the Christian hope of 'Heaven' ridiculous by saying they do not want 'to spend eternity playing harps'. The answer to such people is that if they cannot understand books written for grown-ups, they should not talk about them."[143]

Does that seem too harsh? It probably is for most of us in most of our situations. But bear in mind the dramatic differences between the contexts we inhabit (usually one-on-one conversations with a friend) and Lewis's platforms (radio broadcasts, public speeches, or arguments in books). It fits some situations to make sweeping or pointed declarations. But when sitting across the table from a friend, we should temper the boldness of our rebukes.

Our gentle pushbacks need to be both genuinely gentle and genuine pushbacks. At this point, some self-reflection is in order. Some people's natural response to conflict is to attack back. Others withdraw or acquiesce. Which are you?

Of the two standard responses—fight or flight—which is your default mode?

For those of us who are quick to strike back, we should ask God to help us listen longer and respond more gently. Using introductory phrases like these can help:

"It seems to me that…"
"I wonder if…"
"I think we could consider that…"
"That's one way of thinking about it. What do you think of…?"

If, on the other hand, we tend to go silent in particular situations or with particular people, we can start by asking God for wisdom and boldness. We can try beginning with brief statements like "I disagree" or "I'm not so sure" or "Can we discuss that?"

We all need to find ways to disagree without discord. That's no easy task in today's culture of lashing back through social media ("anti-social media" sometimes seems more apt) and "drop the mic" putdowns. Perhaps the greatest displays of grace show up as "a gentle answer [that] turns away wrath" instead of the more frequently screeched "harsh word [that] stirs up anger" (Proverbs 15 v 1).

## READING THE TIMES

We now need to consider responses to objections specific to our current day. Lewis understood his times well and responded brilliantly. One of his most substantive rebukes—and one that's particularly relevant today—was his condemnation of chronological snobbery. This view asserts that what we believe today must be true because it's most recent. The assumption is that we've evolved intellectually so our beliefs must be better than those of less enlightened people of the past.

Lewis returned to this theme many times, knowing that you sometimes have to undermine assumptions before you offer alternatives. Lewis knew the power of chronological snobbery because he himself was held captive by it for years. He dismissed Christianity simply because he saw it as outdated.

Don't you know people who feel the same way about aspects of our faith today? "It's so archaic," they might say. "Today, we're more advanced in our thinking, more scientific, more rational," they might add. Our pre-evangelistic tactic, at that point, needs to chip away at the chronological snobbery behind their unexamined assumptions. It can sound like this:

> "You say you don't believe in hell because it's an outdated idea. Is that right? Do you think it's stupid? I wonder: do you think Jesus was stupid? He spoke more about hell than anyone else in the Bible."

Or:

> "You reject the idea of eternal life in heaven. You think we only live on in people's memories. Am I understanding you correctly? I agree that we live on in people's memories and their hearts. But is that enough? If we just die, get buried, and turn into fertilizer, does that give us any basis for hope? Do you ever wonder if there's something more?"

Or:

> "You reject Christianity because, you say, Christians are hypocrites. I've heard you say, 'At least I'm not a hypocrite' many times. Is that the worst sin—hypocrisy? Aren't there worse things? And do you think *all* Christians are hypocrites? Are there more Christian hypocrites than non-Christian hypocrites?"

Not all objections to the gospel consist of this level of thought. We live in a time of shallow slogans and trite clichés. Some people seem to build their lives on jargon like "You just have to believe in yourself" or "You don't find yourself; you create yourself" or "What's true for you isn't necessarily true for me." Again, we need to push back. Some clichés need to crumble before deep thought can engage.

It's worth brainstorming in advance how you might do that. I sometimes simply say, "Really?" or "Can we discuss that?" or "What does that phrase mean to you?" A few short responses like these can be enough to break through the walls of slogans.

Similarly, sometimes we need to question the question before we answer it. This takes some practice, but I am convinced it is a skill we can all develop.

For example, if someone asks you, "Are you saying atheists don't go to heaven just because they don't believe in God?" you might reply, "Why would an atheist want to go to heaven?" They might look confused by your response, but don't let confusion on their part prompt discouragement on your part. Sometimes people must feel perplexed before they open up to another perspective. We could follow up with "I don't understand why someone who has lived their whole life apart from God would want to spend eternity with that God." I would not quote C.S. Lewis to them at this point, but his insight can shape our perspective: "There are only two kinds of people in the end: those who say to God, 'Thy will be done,' and those to whom God says, in the end, '*Thy* will be done.'"[144]

Or if someone asks why you don't believe in karma—the view that our deeds in this life will impact the shape of our future lives—you might ask, "Does that sound good to you?" Again, you should anticipate a response of confusion—mostly because few ever challenge anyone's religious views. You can expand with "If this life amounts to our paying for something we did in a previous life, it doesn't seem that there's much hope for things to ever get better. It sounds devoid of hope or redemption or grace."

Or if people ask you (often with a fair amount of condemnation) if you're trying to convert them, you might push back with "It sounds as if you're trying to convert *me*." They'll feel horrified by this accusation. But they must come to admit they want to convert you to a kind of Christianity that doesn't try to convert people! Their efforts to convert you are just as pointed as your efforts to convert them. Of course, you could try a different tactic and shock them with "Of course I'm trying to convert you! What kind of Christian would I be if I didn't try? Jesus made that his final commandment to his followers—to make disciples of everyone." If they soften just a bit, you might add, "Doesn't everyone try to tell others about good things they've found? 'You must try this new restaurant' or 'You've got to go see that movie.' Wouldn't we want people to tell us if they've found something really great?"

As we counter common clichés and objections, we must continue to remember that these challenges need to be delivered gently with heavy doses of kindness and drastic reductions in volume. We're trying to help people move toward the truth, not drive them away from it.

## SOBER WARNINGS

There's one more variety of Lewis's pushbacks worthy of consideration. Sometimes he critiqued behaviors as well as beliefs. He looked intently at how sinful hearts go in deadly directions. He warned people to turn back before it was too late. These pushbacks often appeared in his fiction, like the way he portrayed Eustace turning into a dragon because of his greed (see earlier discussion in chapter 6).

Some of his most stinging rebukes cross the stage in his fantastic drama *The Great Divorce*. A series of characters in hell introduce themselves and reveal how they arrived in that damned situation. We see what pride, anger, bitterness, and lust turn into when left unchecked for all eternity. It reminds us of Lewis's warning about hell:

> *"Now there are a good many things which would not be worth bothering about if I were going to live only seventy years, but which I had better bother about very seriously if I am going to live forever. Perhaps my bad temper or my jealousy are gradually getting worse—so gradually that the increase in seventy years will not be very noticeable. But it might be absolute hell in a million years: in fact, if Christianity is true, Hell is the precisely correct technical term for what it would be."* [145]

Once you've read about the grumbling woman in *The Great Divorce*, you never forget her. Her entire appearance occurs on just a single page—filled as one long, breathless string of complaints. Then comes Lewis's evaluation of her malady: "The question is whether she is a grumbler, or only a grumble. If there is a real woman—even the least trace of one—still there inside the grumbling, it can be brought to life again." [146]

My point is that sometimes our evangelistic conversations need to have elements of warning in them. If heeded, they can help people turn away from sin and run toward the Savior. We need to find our voice to say, "I'm concerned about you" or "Please don't dismiss what I'm about to say" or "I really hope you'll rethink your beliefs" or "I fear for what you may become if you keep heading down this path."

I do realize this task involves much discomfort. But we must keep front and center in our minds that our highest goal in evangelism is God's glory, not our comfort. We need to care more about another person's soul than about our own solace. Long-term gain (theirs) outweighs short-term pain (ours).

During my second year in college, when I was searching for God (although I didn't identify it as such at the time), I wrote a letter to the friend who had given me a copy of the New Testament. He was the one who encouraged me to read *Mere Christianity*. I told him how happy I was now that I'd finally declared music as my major. I wrote, "I believe this is what I've been searching for. Perhaps I'll find that one piece of music that will satisfy me." He wrote back a very kind letter, mostly expressing how happy he was about my choosing my major. But he added, "You know I love music and have found immense pleasure in it. But I do not think music can provide what you're looking for. I know quite a few very disappointed musicians who thought their music could provide what only God can deliver. I don't think you'll feel satisfied until you look to God through Jesus."

I was furious! How dare he "rain on my parade" of the joy of selecting a major. Yet something inside told me he might be right. Of course, he was. I still have that letter.

Sometimes, the most kind, helpful, and loving words you can say are "I disagree."

# 10. THE CALL TO RESPOND

There is a time for every evangelistic situation,
    And a season for every witnessing activity under the
    heavens:
A time to sow and a time to reap,
A time to answer questions and a time to pose questions,
A time to appeal to clues and a time to proclaim truths,
A time to respond clearly and a time to push back gently,
A time to stir uneasiness and a time to stoke the imagination,
A time to pray and a time to resist attacks,
A time to offer reasons and a time to call for a response.

After four weeks of sowing through his radio broadcasts, C.S. Lewis sought to reap. In the fifth talk (the chapter of *Mere Christianity* entitled "We Have Cause to Be Uneasy") he said, "When you know you are sick, you will listen to the doctor." He then briefly restated the gospel—that we can't meet the demands of the law but that they have been met for us—and added, "All I am doing is to ask people to face the facts—to understand the question which Christianity claims to answer. And they are very terrifying facts. I wish it was possible to say something more agreeable. But I must say what I think true."[147]

Note how far he came in just five short radio broadcasts, less than 30 pages in the written form—from "right and wrong as a clue to the meaning of the universe" to "we have cause to be uneasy." Yet, if we're honest, we must acknowledge that Lewis's call for a response was not strong enough—at least, not yet.

He went further at the end of his second series of broadcasts. In the chapter entitled "The Practical Conclusion," he warned about the judgment at Jesus' second coming: "Christians think He is going to land in force; we do not know when. But we can guess why He is delaying. He wants to give us the chance of joining His side freely…When that happens, it is the end of the world … It will be too late then to choose your side. There is no use saying you choose to lie down when it has become impossible to stand up … Now, today, this moment, is our chance to choose the right side."[148]

At the end of his fourth and last series of broadcasts, he offered his strongest appeal:

> *"Give up yourself, and you will find your real self. Lose your life and you will save it. Submit to death, death of your ambitions and favourite wishes every day and death of your whole body in the end: submit with every fibre of your being, and you will find eternal life. Keep back nothing. Nothing that you have not given away will be really yours. Nothing in you that has not died will ever be raised from the dead. Look for yourself, and you will find in the long run only hatred, loneliness, despair, rage, ruin, and decay. But look for Christ and you will find Him, and with Him everything else thrown in."* [149]

## A VITAL STEP

Sooner or later, we need to shift from clarifying to calling. We present the gospel, answer questions, offer illustrations, and provide other aids for conveying the good news. But then, we risk discomfort and say, "Are you ready to become a Christian?" This may never feel comfortable or natural. But it is indispensable.

It is not difficult to marshal a list of Bible passages that include a call to respond *as part of* the message of salvation. Everyone needs more than knowledge of some historical facts about Jesus' death or some theological answers to theoretical questions. Everyone must repent and believe.

The primacy of repentance appears at the beginning of John the Baptist's ministry, when he declares, "Repent, for the kingdom of heaven has come near" (Matthew 3 v 2). Likewise, Jesus inaugurates his earthly preaching ministry with "The kingdom of God has come near. Repent and believe the good news!" (Mark 1 v 15) And at the culmination of Peter's Pentecost sermon, he calls people to "repent and be baptized, every one of you, in the name of Jesus Christ for the forgiveness of your sins" (Acts 2 v 38).

Jesus turned from teaching to calling for a response at key moments. After asking his disciples for polling results about his identity ("Who do people say I am?"), he pointedly asked, "But what about you? ... Who do you say I am?" (Mark 8 v 28-29) After boldly announcing, "I am the resurrection and the life. The one who believes in me will live, even though they die; and whoever lives by believing in me will never die," he added words that often get overlooked: "Do you believe this?" (John 11 v 26).

We must remember these passages and allow them to dig deeply into the marrow of our evangelistic bones. Search the Scriptures and see these frequent calls to respond. Feel the force of them because when temptations to compromise come along (and they *will* come), you will feel the draw to just "be a silent witness" or "not be a fanatic" or embrace the flawed slogan that says, "Preach the gospel at all times; when necessary, use words."[150]

## COUNTING THE COST

One mistake many of us make is never getting around to pivoting our gospel conversations from discussions to decisions. Eventually, we must point people away from our interpersonal dialogues to their interactions directly with God. Everyone needs to call upon the name of the Lord to be saved (Romans 10 v 13). So we need to urge them to do so.

If you've never or rarely invited someone to trust in Christ's cross-work for their salvation, ask yourself why. Do you fear rejection? Do you idolize your own comfort above God's glory? (That's my go-to idolatry, I regret to admit.) The same attitude that brought you into the kingdom—repentance— may help set you free to confidently call for responses.

The opposite mistake is to push too hard for a response when someone is not ready. We can be in danger of sounding angry or harsh or condescending. "You're a sinner!" or "What are you waiting for?" might not help people to cross from darkness to light.

Do you fall into that trap? What is it that prompts you to push too hard? Is it impatience with God's timing? Lack of trust in his power to convict? Overconfidence in your own role in the evangelism process? Repentance may be in order for you as well.

A third, more subtle mistake is to fall prey to the rather common temptation of lowering the bar too far to "get people in." We want so desperately for them to come to faith that we downplay the cost of discipleship and distort our message.

We can fall into this trap in several ways. For example, we might tell people that salvation is as simple as accepting a gift being handed to them. The New Testament does indeed compare salvation to receiving a gift (Ephesians 2 v 8-9). But the gift of salvation differs drastically from a birthday present. True, both are unmerited. But receiving the birthday present doesn't involve repentance of sins or acknowledging inability to provide the gift for oneself. Author and New Testament scholar Dane Ortlund sums up the doctrine of justification beautifully: "It is the most counterintuitive aspect of Christianity, that we are declared right with God not once we begin to get our act together but when we collapse into honest acknowledgment that we never will."[151] So, be careful about using the gift illustration too loosely. Perhaps the illustration of giving a drowning person a life preserver works better. They still have to receive it, but it feels more like salvation than a birthday present.

Whatever illustration we may choose, we always need to bring the discussion back to where the illustrations point—to the innocent Messiah who suffered so sinners can be saved. Otherwise we will risk presenting a version of Christianity that is not the true one at all.

It is this mistake that C.S. Lewis especially helps us to avoid. He provides numerous models to help us urge hearers to understand the cost and significance of repenting and believing in Christ. Lewis does not downplay the need for repentance or the desperate situation of sinners without Christ. We need to follow his example and tell people they are "not simply an imperfect creature who needs improvement [but] … a rebel who must lay down his arms."[152]

Lewis helped people count the cost by sharing honestly about his own resistance to the gospel. For example, he spoke of not "caring for" the Sermon on the Mount. "I suppose no one 'cares for' it. Who can *like* being knocked flat on his face by a sledge-hammer?"[153] Or imagine how an atheist might admit his anger when hearing Lewis recount, "I maintained that God did not exist. I was also very angry with God for not existing."[154] When people heard of Lewis's doubts, questions, and objections—followed by his account of submitting to Christ's lordship—they could imagine themselves following his lead.

We can do the same. What was your own journey to faith like? What held you back? What did "repentance and belief" look like for you—and what changed once you received Christ? Was there a sudden crisis or a gradual movement into trusting Jesus as Lord? Don't be afraid to use your own story to help others imagine themselves taking this most important of steps.

Of course, the cost and change are not just present when someone first becomes a Christian. Lewis cautioned people against costless discipleship—throughout the Christian life—in various ways. After reading *The Lion, the Witch and the Wardrobe*, I doubt anyone can forget the warning that Aslan isn't safe. "'Safe?' said Mr. Beaver; '…Who said anything about safe? 'Course he isn't safe. But he's good. He's the King, I tell you.'"[155] More directly, Lewis taught, "It is just no good asking God to make us happy in our own way without bothering about religion. God cannot give us a happiness and peace apart from Himself, because it is not there. There is no such thing."[156] Still even more pointedly, he flashed these warning lights: "Christ says 'Give me All. I don't want so much of your time and so much of your money and so much of your work: I want You. I have not come to torment your natural self, but to kill it.'"[157]

Lewis never wavered in expressing the severity of the need to surrender. Nor should we. After all, Jesus equated following him with "taking up [a] cross"—a sure symbol of death. He added, "Whoever finds their life will lose it, and whoever loses their life for my sake will find it" (Matthew 10 v 38-39).

But that doesn't mean we must sound stern all the time. In a public forum, Lewis was once asked, "Which of the religions of the world gives to its followers the greatest happiness?" He responded, "While it lasts, the religion of worshipping oneself is the best. I have an elderly acquaintance of about eighty, who has lived a life of unbroken selfishness and self-admiration from the earliest years, and is, more or less, I regret to say, one of the happiest men I know. From the moral point of view it is very difficult! I am not approaching the question from that angle. As you perhaps know, I haven't always been a Christian. I didn't go to religion to make me happy. I always knew a bottle of Port would do that. If you want a religion to make you feel really comfortable, I certainly don't recommend Christianity."[158]

Sometimes humor can help.

## CHOOSING OUR WORDS

As we prepare to call people to respond, it's worth thinking about vocabulary wisely, crafting phrases ahead of time, rather than relying on spontaneous creativity. When someone is ready to believe, that is not the time to search for words. You'll want to practice what to say before then.

Maybe you'll feel confident to use imagery like Lewis— telling your hearers, "Choose a side" or "Lay down [your] arms" or "Give up yourself." The Scriptures can help a great deal with this. I personally find it useful to turn to John 3 v 1-21, which tells the story of Jesus' conversation with Nicodemus. It zeroes in on the need for a response and explains what that entails—using the image of rebirth and a comparison between the Spirit and wind. All the imagery we need is already there for us in Jesus' words. I generally read the passage together with the person: I have them read it out loud, ask questions to see if they understand it, and clarify whatever needs explaining. Then I ask them if they're ready to respond in the way Jesus encouraged Nicodemus to respond.[159]

It's also well worth thinking carefully about the specific terms we are using when we're not looking directly at a Bible passage.

The word "respond" serves us well—better than "decide," a notion which shines the spotlight more on ourselves. When we ask people to respond, we focus on what God has done.

The phrase "becoming a Christian" is also useful because it conveys the reality of rebirth or re-creation. This points to more than a cognitive change of beliefs. When people consider becoming something new, it moves them toward surrendering their entire being, not just their minds.

"Believe" may need translation in some current contexts. Many people think belief involves pretending something is true that really isn't. Or that by believing something, you make it true. To explain to people what the Bible means by "believe," I like to substitute the word "trust." When we believe in Jesus, we transfer our trust from ourselves to him. Once again, we stop relying on what we do and rest, instead, on what he did.

I like to ask the question "Is there anything holding you back from trusting Christ right now?" This encourages people to embrace the gospel with their whole selves. The contrasting images of "holding back" and "trusting" can release their grasp on things that blockade belief. The very way we word the question helps move them from outside to inside.

"Receive" also appears in Scripture (for example John 1 v 12) as a synonym for "believe." Like "believe," it may need some translation or defining. But, for some people, the notion of receiving something implies a kind of surrender or submission—like receiving a pardon in a court of law.

## WE NEED TO RESPOND, TOO

So far, we have examined the non-Christian's need to respond to the gospel. But the gospel also calls *us, Christians,* to respond by committing to proclaim the message that alone offers salvation.

We dare not hide behind excuses like "We're *only* called to witness silently with our lives" or "We *only* need to tell of our experience." This may start the process. But we must never omit the part of the message that calls people to repent and believe.

This is difficult. We must admit the difficulty, face it square on, and warn people of the dire consequences of their unbelief. We have good reason to expect pain in this process—both for them and for us. In addition to the likelihood of rejection from them (as we explored in chapter 7) we can expect something equally painful: "great sorrow and unceasing anguish in [our] heart[s]" if people don't respond (Romans 9 v 2). But that must not stop us.

C.S. Lewis's example can help us again here. He could have stayed sequestered in his academic classrooms, private studies, or at his writing desk. He lectured with prowess and impressed large gatherings of captivated students. But he stepped out from the ivory tower of academia to preach on the radio, at military bases, and in other situations. He chose to adapt his vocabulary, manner, and delivery to fit a much broader audience. He took his own advice: "I have come to the conviction that if you cannot translate your thoughts into uneducated language, then your thoughts were confused. Power to translate is the test of having really understood one's own meaning."[160]

Thus we see that, as a scholar, he could write complex propositions like "Sometimes, when a community is comparatively homogeneous and comparatively undisturbed over a long period, such a system of belief can continue, of course with development, long after material culture has progressed far beyond the level of savagery."[161]

But, as an evangelist, he could pointedly say, "'Make no mistake,' He [God] says, 'if you let me, I will make you perfect. The moment you put yourself in My hands, that is what you are in for. Nothing less, or other, than that."[162]

And so, just as non-Christians need to trust God's power to save them through the gospel, Christians need to trust God's power to use them to preach the gospel. Few can craft words as brilliantly as Lewis. But all Christians, even those with the weakest of language skills, can be used by God in astonishing ways. We need to put ourselves in God's hands and open our mouths, risking rejection to tell people of the only hope they have.

They may ignore us, argue against us, or tell us to never bring that topic up again. But what if they do respond in faith?! What if—after hearing our arguments, clues, illustrations, clarifications, and explanations—they say, "Yes!" What then? They'll be saved! Born again! Adopted! Redeemed! Reconciled! Justified! They'll be new creations! They'll have eternal life! "The door on which [they] have been knocking all [their] lives will open at last."[163]

Or, as Lewis put it in another place, they will "be loved by God, not merely pitied, but delighted in as an artist delights in his work or a father in a son—it seems impossible, a weight or burden of glory which our thoughts can hardly sustain. But so it is."[164]

# CONCLUSION: STOPPING TO STARE

We've come a long way—from clues that point to "another world" to surrendering to the King of that world. And that's appropriate because many people today need to come a long way from clinging to "second things" to finding the only "first thing" that can save.

At the very end of C.S. Lewis's account of his journey from atheism to Christianity, *Surprised by Joy*, he revisited that life-long theme of joy. He wrote:

> *"But what, in conclusion, of Joy? For that, after all, is what the story has mainly been about. To tell you the truth, the subject has lost nearly all interest for me since I became a Christian ... I now know that the experience, considered as a state of my own mind, had never had the kind of importance I once gave it. It was valuable only as a pointer to something other and outer."* [165]

But here is an irony that Lewis found, echoing Ecclesiastes, the Sermon on the Mount, and other places in Scripture. When people set first and second things in proper order, they can enjoy the second things as gifts from God, at whose "right hand are pleasures forevermore" (Psalm 16 v 11, ESV).

They don't totally lose those "pointers." (Of course, they *do* need to totally abandon sinful behavior.) Instead, they now see second things in their proper perspective. That's why Lewis wrote this as the very last sentence of *Surprised by Joy*: "Not, of course, that I don't often catch myself stopping to stare at roadside objects of even less importance."[166]

This was no relapse on Lewis's part but a profound reappraisal. His "stopping to stare" now comes as appropriate appreciation, not idolatrous worship.

When people respond in faith to the gospel, they find salvation, peace, and eternal life. If they had attached their hopes to success or relationships or possessions or approval from others or countless other "pointers," they now find shelter in God himself, their Rock and Redeemer. They can stop and stare and "see the land as it really is."[167] They can enjoy "things ... all day long without [God's] minding in the least—sleeping, washing, eating, drinking, making love, playing, praying, working."[168] They "find Him, and with Him everything else thrown in."[169] They "seek first his kingdom and his righteousness, and all these things [are] given to [them] as well" (Matthew 6 v 33).

It seems appropriate to "stop and stare" in several directions and ask God to use our gazing not only as a pointer to the gospel but also as preparation for fruitful mere evangelism.

First, stop and stare inside you. Recall the joy of your salvation: how God sovereignly worked to adopt you. What aspect of the gospel drew you in at first? Was it forgiveness or God's presence or becoming part of the body of Christ or something else? If you've been a Christian since early childhood, what aspect of the gospel seems most meaningful to you *now*?

Look within and see how God has gifted you to enhance your efforts to reach out to non-Christians. What passions and interests do you share with them? Where have you found joy, as Lewis described it—those unsatisfied desires that point to a different world?

When I became a Christian, I did not lose my love for music. On the contrary, it has only grown over the years. Now, when a piece of music concludes, I actually enjoy the letdown. It reminds me that music is supposed to disappoint and it intensifies my longing for eternity. No longer looking to music to save me, I can enjoy it as a pointer to the Giver of all good gifts. And I can point others toward that same God. Music has become a frequent go-to topic to start pre-evangelistic conversations.

Second, stop and stare at the Christians around you and the local church in which God has placed you. How might you fit on a team for evangelism—one that can reach a wide variety of people? Remember that Lewis thought he played only one role in outreach: that of an apologist who made a coherent case to consider. Someone else needed to come along and preach more pointedly for a response. How do you see yourself in the evangelistic process? Share these ideas with other Christians and ask them to join you in reaching out.

Third, stop and stare at the world around you. Who has God sovereignly placed in your nooks of his world—where you live, work, or play? What spiritual beliefs do those people have? How firmly do they hold them? What topics might start discussions and build bridges for the gospel? What clues about God do you see in everyday life?

What system do you have (or could you start having) to pray regularly for those around you? Try to develop ways to see people as Lewis saw them: "There are no *ordinary* people. You have never talked to a mere mortal. Nations, cultures, arts, civilizations—these are mortal, and their life is to us as the life of a gnat. But it is immortals whom we joke with, work with, marry, snub, and exploit—immortal horrors or everlasting splendours."[170]

Fourth, stop and stare at C.S. Lewis. Reflect and identify which lessons you particularly want to apply to your life. Perhaps you've put one or two of his books on your reading list. Take courage from remembering how God used him, a rather unlikely evangelist, in the proclaiming of the gospel.

We do need a word of caution, however. Lewis wasn't perfect and his theology, at certain points, was suspect. Even his great book *Mere Christianity* has some flaws.[171] If I ever give a non-Christian a copy of it, I try to warn them that some of his attitudes are outdated and some of his ideas have weaknesses. In most cases, I suggest people focus on just the first two books of *Mere Christianity* because I think those are the most pertinent.[172] You'll need to decide how you'll use his writings in your efforts to reach out. Will you give friends copies of *The Lion, the Witch and the Wardrobe*? Or *The Screwtape Letters*? Or *Mere Christianity*? Some people respond better to fiction than nonfiction. Make some decisions ahead of time so you'll know what you'll use when the time seems appropriate.

Fortunately, we have a resource far better than C.S. Lewis— the Bible. Thus, fifth, stop and stare at the Scriptures, especially their countless depictions of the gospel. Read, study, memorize, meditate, and feast on God's word. Dig deeply into the Old Testament's preparations, predictions, and foreshadowings of the gospel. Examine closely the New Testament's exposition of all that Jesus said and did. Allow God's "two-edged sword" to transform you so others will want to read that same book—the one that has made such a difference in your life.

For some of us who struggle with evangelistic hesitancy (yes, I include myself in that camp), remembering what Scripture says about us may free up our voices. God "uses us to spread the aroma of the knowledge of him everywhere. For we are to God the pleasing aroma of Christ among those who are being saved and those who are perishing. To the one we are an aroma that brings death; to the other, an aroma that brings life" (2 Corinthians 2 v 14-16). God is not limited by less than perfect messengers. Our confidence is in him, not ourselves.

Most important, stop and stare at the Lord himself. Marvel at his power and grace. Listen to people's stories of how God rescued them and delight in how he worked. Nothing is impossible for him. No one is so lost that God can't find, rescue, and redeem them. Make the sharing of testimonies a regular component of your church's small-group gatherings or other times of fellowship. It's easy to lose sight of what God did many years ago and grow complacent or bored. Don't let that happen.

I've spent more than half of my life in evangelistic ministry. I've seen God work in ways that can only be described as utterly miraculous. I've listened to people wonder about meaning in life and how to know God. I've sat face to face with atheists, agnostics, people of other faiths, and young adults struggling with all sorts of temptations and consequences of destructive choices. I've heard many expressions of unbelief—like this letter written by a seventeen-year-old student to a friend:

> *"You ask me my religious views: you know, I think, that I believe in no religion. There is absolutely no proof for any of them, and from a philosophical standpoint Christianity is not even the best. All religions, that is, all mythologies, to give them their proper name, are merely man's own invention—Christ as much as Loki ... Superstition of course in every age has held the common people, but in every age the educated and thinking ones have stood outside it, though usually outwardly conceded to it for convenience ... Of course, mind you, I am not laying down as a*

*certainty that there is nothing outside the material world: considering the discoveries that are always being made, this would be foolish … Whenever any new light can be got as to such matters, I will be glad to welcome it. In the meantime I am not going to go back to the bondage of believing in any old (and already decaying) superstition."*

You should know that this letter could have been written by any one of thousands, maybe millions of people today (although probably not so eloquently). An increasing percentage of our neighbors, friends, and co-workers identify themselves as having no religion at all. Like the writer of this letter, they feel intellectually and morally superior to Christians who believe "mythologies of their own invention" or "superstitions." You should know that many people embrace these kinds of thoughts with deep-seated conviction, even if they don't say them out loud.

But you should also know that that letter was written by C.S. Lewis,[173] the one who called himself "the most reluctant convert."[174] And perhaps this is the most important lesson we can learn from his life, experiences, books, essays, letters, and friendships: "Surely the arm of the LORD is not too short to save" (Isaiah 59 v 1).

Let's stop and stare in one last direction—toward heaven. People who respond in faith to the gospel, as C.S. Lewis did, realize God's "compulsion is our liberation,"[175] and will join that "great multitude that no one could count, from every nation, tribe, people and language, standing before the throne and before the Lamb. They [will be] wearing white robes and [will be] holding palm branches in their hands. And they [will cry] out in a loud voice: 'Salvation belongs to our God, who sits on the throne, and to the Lamb'" (Revelation 7 v 9-10).

They will dwell where God "'will wipe every tear from their eyes. There will be no more death' or mourning or crying or pain, for the old order of things has passed away" (Revelation 21 v 4).

They will begin "Chapter One of the Great Story which no one on earth has read: which goes on for ever: in which every chapter is better than the one before."[176]

# ACKNOWLEDGMENTS

C.S. Lewis played a major role in my coming to faith in Jesus, the Son of God (because, as Lewis taught me, he was not a "lunatic on the level of a person who calls himself a poached egg"). Thus, I'm so thankful for Rich Van Pelt, who first quoted Lewis to me and continued to do so as I moved closer and closer to saving faith. Marshall Taylor and Ron Thomas, two other C.S. Lewis fans, pointed me to Lewis's works in my earliest days as a believer. We experienced Lewisian "joy" during those formative Bible studies where we studied Romans, referenced Lewis, and drank gallons of iced tea around Mort and Jeanne Lowenstein's dining-room table.

I'm so glad Tim Thornborough thought that the idea for this book was worth pursuing, when I first mentioned it to him in a pub in Edinburgh. His encouragement helped tremendously and Katy Morgan, my editor at The Good Book Company, made this a much better book with her expertise.

Several friends read parts of the book and offered keen insights—Mark Petersburg, Spencer Brand, Jake Fritzke, Aaron Welty, Ben Hein, Rob Yancey, and Greg Boros all saw things I had missed and suggested things I had forgotten. You are all such good friends.

A band of brothers prayed for me as I wrote. God used their intercessions in ways Lewis endorsed in his *Letters to Malcolm*. Thank you Dan Strull, Glenn Oeland, Jim

Dempsey, Jeff Thornhill, Don Knox, and Carl Meyer. Bill Kynes read every word and patiently shined his keen theological light on places where I needed to clarify.

Our Fairfax Community Group at Capital Presbyterian Church prayed me through the struggle of writing—even through a pandemic.

Lyle Dorsett's lifelong scholarship of Lewis and his kind friendship to me over the years combined to propel me with energy to write this book.

I am especially grateful to God for The C. S. Lewis Institute, where I have been able to hang my hat for many years. Joel Woodruff, Tom Simmons, Tom Tarrants, Jake Fritzke, Semy Godo, our Board, and all our City Directors make for a stimulating and fun environment that supports me in ways not unlike the ways in which "The Inklings" helped Lewis.

I dedicate this book to my wife, Pam, who listens so patiently to all my ideas and helps me see which ones should make it into a book and which ones should never go beyond my study. God's word is wonderful and true: "He who finds a wife finds what is good and receives favor from the LORD" (Proverbs 18 v 22).

# NOTES

## INTRODUCTION
1 www.christianitytoday.com/ct/2000/april24/5.92.html (accessed 27 Nov. 2020).
2 Justin Phillips, *C.S. Lewis in a Time of War* (Zondervan, 2006), p 116.
3 Justin Phillips, *C.S. Lewis in a Time of War,* p 117.
4 George Sayer, *Jack: A Life of C.S. Lewis,* (Crossway, 1988), p 278.
5 C.S. Lewis, *Mere Christianity* (Geoffrey Bles, 1952; this edition, HarperCollins, 1980), p 52.
6 C.S. Lewis, *Mere Christianity,* p 136-137.
7 C.S. Lewis, *Surprised by Joy: The Shape of My Early Life* (Geoffrey Bles, 1955; this edition, Mariner Books, 2012), p 228-229.
8 C.S. Lewis, *God in the Dock* (Eerdmans, 1970), p 183.
9 C.S. Lewis, *God in the Dock,* p 181.
10 Martin Moynihan, ed. *The Latin Letters of C.S. Lewis* (St. Augustine Press, 1987), p 101. Quoted in Lyle W. Dorsett, *Seeking the Secret Place: The Spiritual Formation of C.S. Lewis* (Brazos, 2004), p 28.

## 1. THE NECESSITY OF PRE-EVANGELISM
11 Thomas A. Tarrants, *Consumed by Hate: Redeemed by Love* (Nelson Books, 2019), p 117.
12 Abigail Santamaria, *Joy: Poet, Seeker, and the Woman Who Captivated C.S. Lewis,* (Houghton, Mifflin, Harcourt, 2015), p 175.
13 I explore this topic at much greater length in my other books *Questioning Evangelism* (Kregel, 2004, 2017), *Bringing the*

*Gospel Home* (Crossway, 2011), and *Unlikely Converts* (Kregel, 2020). We also have much to learn on this topic from Francis Schaeffer. See especially his *The Francis A. Schaeffer Trilogy* (Crossway, 1990).

14 John R.W. Stott, *The Message of Acts* (InterVarsity Press, 1999), p 290.

15 C.S. Lewis, *Mere Christianity*, p 3.

16 This phrase comes from the title of the first "book" of *Mere Christianity*.

17 W.H. Lewis, *Letters of C.S. Lewis* (Harcourt Brace, 1966), p 359.

18 C.S. Lewis, letter of 10 February, 1941, quoted in Angus J.L. Menuge, ed., *C.S. Lewis: Lightbearer in the Shadowlands* (Crossway, 1997), p 213.

19 C.S. Lewis, *God in the Dock*, p 243.

20 C.S. Lewis, *God in the Dock*, p 94-95.

21 C.S. Lewis, *God in the Dock*, p 90-91.

22 C.S. Lewis, *God in the Dock*, p 172.

23 C.S. Lewis, *Mere Christianity*, p 25.

24 C.S. Lewis, *God in the Dock*, p 99.

25 C.S. Lewis, *Surprised by Joy*, p 181.

26 C.S. Lewis, *Surprised by Joy*, p 170.

27 Paul Ford, ed., *Yours, Jack: Spiritual Direction from C.S. Lewis* (HarperCollins, 2008), p 28.

28 Paul Ford, *Yours, Jack*, p 27.

29 C.S. Lewis, *Surprised by Joy*, p 239, 237.

30 I am indebted to Tim Downs' seminal book *Finding Common Ground: How to Communicate with Those Outside the Christian Community...While We Still Can* (Moody, 1999) for my appreciation of the task of sowing.

31 Tim Downs, *Finding Common Ground*, p 18.

## 2. THE APPEAL TO CLUES

32 C.S. Lewis, *Surprised by Joy*, p 17.

33 C.S. Lewis, *The Weight of Glory and Other Addresses* (Geoffrey Bles, 1949; this edition, HarperCollins, 1976), p 42.

34 C.S. Lewis, *The Weight of Glory*, p 39.

35 C.S. Lewis, *The Weight of Glory*, p 31.

36 C.S. Lewis, *Surprised by Joy*, p 17-18.

37 C.S. Lewis, *Surprised by Joy*, p 7.

38 C.S. Lewis, *Of Other Worlds: Essays and Stories* (Geoffrey Bles, 1966; this edition, Harvest Books, 2002), p v.

39 C.S. Lewis, *God in the Dock*, p 12.

40 C.S. Lewis, *The Weight of Glory*, p 140.

41 Gerard Manley Hopkins, "God's Grandeur" in *The Major Works* (Oxford University Press, 2009), p 128.

42 C.S. Lewis, *God in the Dock*, p 280.

43 C.S. Lewis, *The Weight of Glory*, p 30-31.

44 C.S. Lewis, *Mere Christianity*, p 6.

45 George Marsden, *C.S. Lewis's Mere Christianity: A Biography* (Princeton University Press, 2016), p 169.

46 C.S. Lewis, *The Weight of Glory*, p 42.

## 3. THE HONORING OF OBJECTIONS

47 C.S. Lewis, *Surprised by Joy*, p 134.

48 C.S. Lewis, *Mere Christianity*, p 153.

49 C.S. Lewis, *Mere Christianity*, p 9.

50 C.S. Lewis, *God in the Dock*, p 98.

51 James Como, *C.S. Lewis: A Very Short Introduction* (Oxford University Press, 2019), p 109.

52 C.S. Lewis, *Mere Christianity*, p 35.

53 C.S. Lewis, *Mere Christianity*, p 62.

54 C.S. Lewis, *Mere Christianity*, p 38.

55 C.S. Lewis, *The Problem of Pain* (The Centenary Press, 1940; this edition, HarperCollins, 2001), p 5.

56 C.S. Lewis, *Mere Christianity*, p 41.

57 Justin Phillips, *C.S. Lewis in a Time of War*, p 310.

58 Corbin Scott Carnell, "Longing, Reason and the Moral Law in C.S. Lewis's Search" in Alfred J.L. Menuge, ed., *C.S. Lewis, Lightbearer in the Shadowlands*, p 107.

59 See my *Questioning Evangelism* (Kregel, 2004, 2017).

60 This is not the place for a thorough discussion of this complex issue. I am only offering suggestions for ways to approach the topic. For more in-depth responses, see Timothy Keller, *The Reason for God* (Dutton, 2008), p 3-21; Rebecca McLaughlin, *Confronting Christianity* (Crossway, 2019), p 47-58.

61 See Will Herberg, *Protestant Catholic Jew* (Doubleday and Company, 1960).

62 See Paul Rezkalla, "If All Religions Are True, Then God

Is Cruel," *The Gospel Coalition*, March 24, 2014, www.thegospelcoalition.org/article/if-all-religions-are-true-then-god-is-cruel (accessed 9 Dec. 2020).

63 Timothy Keller, *The Reason for God*, p 20.

64 C.S. Lewis, *God in the Dock*, p 98.

## 4. THE STIRRING OF UNEASINESS

65 C.S. Lewis, *Mere Christianity*, p 28.

66 Numbers 14 v 13-20; Nehemiah 9 v 7-18; Psalms 86 v 14-17; 103 v 7-12; 145 v 3-8, Joel 2 v 13-14; Jonah 4 v 1-3; Nahum 1 v 1-3.

67 Alfred Edersheim, *The Life and Times of Jesus the Messiah* (Eerdmans, 1971), p 710-741.

68 See Walter Kaiser, *The Messiah in the Old Testament* (Zondervan, 1995).

69 C.S. Lewis, *The Abolition of Man* (Oxford University Press, 1943; this edition, Touchstone, 1996), p 36.

70 C.S. Lewis, *The Abolition of Man*, p 37.

71 C.S. Lewis, *The Weight of Glory*, p 139.

72 C.S. Lewis, *Mere Christianity*, p 8.

73 C.S. Lewis, *God in the Dock*, p 153.

74 C.S. Lewis, *Surprised by Joy*, p 115.

75 Reed Jolley, "Apostle to Generation X: C.S. Lewis and the Future of Evangelism" in Angus J.L. Menuge, ed., *C.S. Lewis, Lightbearer in the Shadowlands*, p 86.

76 C.S. Lewis, *Mere Christianity*, p 31.

77 C.S. Lewis, *Mere Christianity*, p 32.

## 5. THE CENTRALITY OF THE GOSPEL

78 George Marsden, *C.S. Lewis's Mere Christianity: A Biography*, p 187.

79 C.S. Lewis, *Mere Christianity*, p 51.

80 C.S. Lewis, *Mere Christianity*, p 55.

81 C.S. Lewis, *God in the Dock*, p 101.

82 C.S. Lewis, *Mere Christianity*, p 57.

83 C.S. Lewis, *Mere Christianity*, p 58.

84 C.S. Lewis, *God in the Dock*, p 158.

85 C.S. Lewis, *Mere Christianity*, p 27.

86 For example, www.cru.org/us/en/how-to-know-god/would-you-

like-to-know-god-personally.html or www.twowaystolive.com

87 Timothy Keller, "The Gospel in All Its Forms," *Reformed Perspective Magazine*, Volume 12, Number 9, February 28 to March 6, 2010. www.reformedperspectives.org/articles/tim_keller/tim_keller.Gospel.Forms.html (accessed 9 Dec. 2020).

88 Jerry Bridges, *The Discipline of Grace* (NavPress, 2006), p 45.

89 C.S. Lewis, *The Weight of Glory*, p 178-179.


## 6. THE VALUE OF IMAGERY

90 C.S. Lewis, *God in the Dock*, p 219.

91 C.S. Lewis, *On Stories and Other Essays on Literature* (Harvest, 1982), p 53.

92 C.S. Lewis, *The Problem of Pain*, p 91.

93 C.S. Lewis, *The Weight of Glory*, p 26.

94 Walter Hooper, ed., *The Letters of C.S. Lewis to Arthur Greeves (1914-1963): They Stand Together* (Macmillan, 1979), p 566.

95 Michael Ward, "Escape to Wallaby Wood," in Angus J.L. Menuge, ed., *C.S. Lewis, Light-Bearer in the Shadowlands*, p 151.

96 Michael Ward, "Escape to Wallaby Wood," p 152.

97 C.S. Lewis, *On Stories*, p 47.

98 C.S. Lewis, "Bluspels and Flalansferes: A Semantic Nightmare" in Walter Hooper, ed., *Selected Literary Essays* (Cambridge University Press, 1969), p 265.

99 Philip Zaleski and Carol Zaleski, *The Fellowship: The Literary Lives of the Inklings: J.R.R. Tolkien, C.S. Lewis, Owen Barfield, Charles Williams* (Farrar, Straus and Giroux, 2015), p 240.

100 C.S. Lewis, *The Lion, the Witch and the Wardrobe* (Geoffrey Bles, 1950; this edition, *The Chronicles of Narnia*, Collins, 1998), p 184-185.

101 C.S. Lewis, *Mere Christianity*, p 205.

102 C.S. Lewis, *The Weight of Glory*, p 31.

103 Erica Komisar, "Don't Believe in God? Lie to Your Children," The Wall Street Journal, December 5, 2019. www.wsj.com/articles/dont-believe-in-god-lie-to-your-children-11575591658 (accessed Dec. 10 2020).

104 Two valuable resources to help you grow in appreciation for the many aspects of the gospel are Leon Morris, *The Atonement: Its Meaning and Significance* (InterVarsity Press,

1983); and John Stott, *The Cross of Christ* (InterVarsity Press, 1986).

105 Peter Adam, *Hearing God's Words: Exploring Biblical Spirituality* (InterVarsity Press, 2004), p 141.

106 C.S. Lewis, *The Weight of Glory*, p 58.

## 7. THE REALITY OF OPPOSITION

107 Justin Phillips, *C.S. Lewis in a Time of War,* p 222.

108 For example, James Como, *C.S. Lewis: A Very Short Introduction* (Oxford University Press, 2019), p 108.

109 Philip Zaleski & Carol Zaleski, *The Fellowship*, p 431.

110 A very helpful resource that would repay careful reading is Edward T. Welch, *When People are Big and God is Small* (Presbyterian and Reformed, 1997).

111 This topic requires far more space than is appropriate in this book. I address some aspects of homosexuality in *Questioning Evangelism*. A concise presentation of the Bible's teaching on the topic can be found in Kevin DeYoung's *What Does the Bible Really Teach about Homosexuality?* (Crossway, 2015). For a broader discussion about sexuality in general, see Nancy Pearcey's *Love Thy Body: Answering Hard Questions about Life and Sexuality* (Baker, 2018).

112 C.S. Lewis, *Mere Christianity*, p 95.

113 See Michael Kruger, *Christianity at the Crossroads: How the Second Century Shaped the Future of the Church* (InterVarsity Press Academic, 2018).

114 Some of the most valuable resources on this topic come from Christians who identify as "same-sex attracted" while remaining faithful to God's teaching about sexuality. Some of the best are Sam Allberry, *Is God Anti-Gay?* (The Good Book Company, 2013); Ed Shaw, *Same-Sex Attraction and the Church: The Surprising Plausibility of the Celibate Life* (InterVarsity Press, 2015); Rachel Gilson, *Born Again This Way* (The Good Book Company, 2020). Joe Dallas' many books are also very helpful.

115 Clifford A. Morris, "C.S. Lewis Was My Friend," *His*, October, 1978 (Vol. 39, No.1), p 12.

116 C.S. Lewis, *The Screwtape Letters* (Geoffrey Bles, 1942; this edition, Macmillan, 1977), p 62-63.

117 C.S. Lewis, *God in the Dock*, p 103.

118 C.S. Lewis, *The Screwtape Letters*, p xiii. Lewis is quoting an old translation of Psalm 36 v 1.

119 C.S. Lewis, *The Screwtape Letters*, p 98-99.


## 8. THE POWER OF PRAYER

120 C.S. Lewis, *The Problem of Pain*, p 19; *Mere Christianity*, p 141.

121 C.S. Lewis, *The Screwtape Letters*, p 19.

122 C.S. Lewis, *The World's Last Night* (Harvest/HBJ, 1952), p 3.

123 C.S. Lewis, *A Grief Observed* (Bantam, 1980), p 4.

124 Lewis, *Yours, Jack*, p 136.

125 Sheldon Vanauken, *A Severe Mercy* (Harper and Row, 1977), p 101.

126 See Walter Hooper, *C.S. Lewis: A Companion and Guide* (HarperCollins, 1996), p 378-9.

127 C.S. Lewis, *The World's Last Night*, p 9.

128 C.S. Lewis, *The World's Last Night*, p 4.

129 C.S. Lewis, *The World's Last Night*, p 5.

130 C.S. Lewis, *Letters to Malcolm: Chiefly on Prayer* (Geoffrey Bles, 1964; this edition, Harvest/HBJ, 1973), p 59.

131 Timothy Keller, *Prayer: Experiencing Awe and Intimacy with God* (Dutton 2014), p 228.

132 C.S. Lewis, *Letters to Malcolm*, p 113.

133 C.S. Lewis, *Letters to Malcolm*, p 114.

134 C.S. Lewis, *Reflections on the Psalms* (HarperOne Reprint edition, 2017), p 1-2.

135 See D.A. Carson, *Praying with Paul* (Baker, 2015). See especially pages 123-144.

136 Jason Mandryk, *Operation World: The Definitive Prayer Guide to Every Nation* (InterVarsity Press, 2010).

137 C.S. Lewis, *The Screwtape Letters*, p 125-126.


## 9. THE TIMELINESS OF PUSHBACK

138 C.S. Lewis, *Mere Christianity*, p 5.

139 C.S. Lewis, *The Weight of Glory*, p 43-44.

140 C.S. Lewis, *Mere Christianity*, p 92.

141 C.S. Lewis, *Mere Christianity*, p 52.

142 Justin Phillips, *C.S. Lewis in a Time of War*, p 148.

143 C.S. Lewis, *Mere Christianity*, p 137.

144 C.S. Lewis, *The Great Divorce* (Geoffrey Bles, 1946; this edition, Macmillan, 1977), p 72.

145 C.S. Lewis, *Mere Christianity*, p 74.

146 C.S. Lewis, *The Great Divorce*, p 74.

## 10. THE CALL TO RESPOND

147 C.S. Lewis, *Mere Christianity*, p 32.

148 C.S. Lewis, *Mere Christianity*, p 65.

149 C.S. Lewis, *Mere Christianity*, p 226-227.

150 Some people attribute this slogan to Francis of Assisi, but he never said it. In fact, his bold and loud evangelism is well documented. He would have laughed at the notion that it's possible to "preach the gospel" and not use words.

151 Dane Ortlund, *Gentle and Lowly: The Heart of Christ for Sinners and Sufferers* (Crossway, 2020), p 78.

152 C.S. Lewis, *Mere Christianity*, p 56.

153 C.S. Lewis, *God in the Dock*, p 182.

154 C.S. Lewis, *Surprised by Joy*, p 115.

155 C.S. Lewis, *The Lion, The Witch and The Wardrobe*, p 146.

156 C.S. Lewis, *Mere Christianity*, p 50.

157 C.S. Lewis, *Mere Christianity*, p 196.

158 C.S. Lewis, *God in the Dock*, p 58.

159 One helpful resource along similar lines is Rebecca Manley Pippert, *Discovering the Real Jesus: Seven Encounters with Jesus from the Gospel of John* (The Good Book Company, 2016).

160 C.S. Lewis, *God in the Dock*, p 98.

161 C.S. Lewis, *The Discarded Image* (Cambridge University Press, 1964; this edition, Cambridge University Press, 2012), p 1.

162 C.S. Lewis, *Mere Christianity*, p 202.

163 C.S. Lewis, *The Weight of Glory*, p 41.

164 C.S. Lewis, *The Weight of Glory*, p 39.

## CONCLUSION: STOPPING TO STARE

165 C.S. Lewis, *Surprised by Joy*, p 238.

166 C.S. Lewis, *Surprised by Joy*, p 238.

167 C.S. Lewis, *The Pilgrim's Regress* (J.M. Dent, 1933; this edition, Eerdmans, 1981), p 175.

168 C.S. Lewis, *The Screwtape Letters*, p 118.

169 C.S. Lewis, *Mere Christianity*, p 191.

170 C.S. Lewis, *The Weight of Glory*, p 46.
171 Lewis's strengths far outweigh his weaknesses. He masterfully explained people's need for salvation and God's provision for that salvation. But he did write some things that conservative theologians have rightly criticized and evangelical Christians should reject. For example, he hinted that adherents of other religions could "belong to Christ without knowing it" (*Mere Christianity*, p 209).
172 A very nice hardback publication of just Book 2 of *Mere Christianity* is *What Christians Believe* (HarperOne, 2005).
173 C.S. Lewis, *Yours, Jack*, p 2-3.
174 C.S. Lewis, *Surprised by Joy*, p 229.
175 C.S. Lewis, *Surprised by Joy*, p 229.
176 C.S. Lewis, *The Chronicles of Narnia*, p 767.

**RANDY NEWMAN** is the Senior Fellow for Evangelism and Apologetics at The C. S. Lewis Institute in the Washington, DC area. He has also taught at numerous theological seminaries and colleges and has written a number of books and articles about evangelism. After serving for over 30 years with Campus Crusade for Christ, he established Connection Points, a ministry to help Christians engage people's hearts the way Jesus did. He and his wife Pam live in Annandale, VA, and are grateful for their children and a growing number of grandchildren.

**BIBLICAL | RELEVANT | ACCESSIBLE**

At The Good Book Company, we are dedicated to helping Christians and local churches grow. We believe that God's growth process always starts with hearing clearly what he has said to us through his timeless word—the Bible.

Ever since we opened our doors in 1991, we have been striving to produce Bible-based resources that bring glory to God. We have grown to become an international provider of user-friendly resources to the Christian community, with believers of all backgrounds and denominations using our books, Bible studies, devotionals, evangelistic resources, and DVD-based courses.

We want to equip ordinary Christians to live for Christ day by day, and churches to grow in their knowledge of God, their love for one another, and the effectiveness of their outreach.

Call us for a discussion of your needs or visit one of our local websites for more information on the resources and services we provide.

Your friends at The Good Book Company

thegoodbook.com | thegoodbook.co.uk
thegoodbook.com.au | thegoodbook.co.nz
thegoodbook.co.in